The Truth of Our Faith

THE TRUTH OF

Discourses from Holy Scripture

Elder Cleopa

Preface by Archimandrite Joseph
Abbot of Xeropotamou Monastery,
Mount Athos

OUR FAITH

on the Tenets of Christian Orthodoxy

of Romania

Translated from Greek and
edited by Fr. Peter Heers

ISBN: 978-1-63941-000-2

Cover Photo: From the dome of the Catholicon of
Xeropotamou Monastery on Mount Athos, Greece.

Back Cover Photo: Elder Cleopa Ilie,
Sihastria Monastery, Romania.

**All Scriptural quotations are taken from the King James Version, unless otherwise
noted. The translator to better reflect the original Greek text has emended some
quotations. All citations of the Psalms are taken from The Psalter According to the
Seventy, translated from the Septuagint Version of the Old Testament by the Holy
Transfiguration Monastery, Brookline, MA.**

This translation has been made from the Greek edition of this work entitled
Αντιαιρετικοί Διάλογοι and published by *Orthodox Kipseli*, Thessalonica.

To all those who, with pain of heart in a spirit of devotion,
seek, ask, and knock at the Door of Truth incessantly,
until their patient endurance is duly rewarded with
the Pearl of Great Price.

"What do you have to say about today's world?"

"As evil as it is, God has love. If His love were to cease, the
world would be destroyed. The love of God gives birth to
mercy, and with His mercy He covers the whole world today.
'God's compassions are over all His works.' All that God has
created He loves. He does not love sin, for He is not the
cause of it, but He loves men even when they sin."

– Elder Cleopa

CONTENTS

Elder Cleopa visits with Archimandrite Joseph during the latter's 1992 tour of Romania with the largest piece of the True Cross of Christ, which is treasured at Xeropotamou.

PREFACE

by Archimandrite Joseph
Abbot of Xeropotamou Monastery, Mount Athos

> *What is more to be desired than a true father – a father in God?*
> Saint Theodore the Studite (759-826)

In Orthodoxy, spiritual authority derives from experience—the experience of the Uncreated. For this experience, one has to look to the ascetical and mystical environment of solitude, discipleship, fasting, and liturgical prayer, as well as noetic unceasing prayer. This is the milieu of monasticism since the dawn of the fourth Christian century. For the Orthodox Church, monasticism represents its eschatological and prophetic spirit, without which it is found quickly in the perilous strait of perhaps becoming an "exotic" but otherwise secularised "tradition", stripped of its otherworldly credentials.

It is for the most part in Orthodox monasticism that you find those grace-filled spiritual leaders—hermits, abbots, cenobitic monks—who have the gift to guide monastics and laypeople alike through the three stages of Christian perfection: *purification, illumination* and *deification.* They are generically called *elders* (*gerontes* or *startzi*), and they play a pivotal role in maintaining the Church in the expectant and eschatological spirit that prevents our gaze from turning earthward.

In the Orthodox Church, the person of the elder occupies a central and authoritative position. According to Bishop Kallistos of Diokleia,

> *There are, in a sense, two forms of apostolic succession within the life of the Church. First, there is the visible succession of the hierarchy, the unbroken series of bishops in different cities, to which Saint Irenaeus made appeal at the end of the second century. Alongside this, largely hidden, existing on a 'charismatic' rather than official level, there is secondly the apostolic succession of the spiritual fathers and mothers in each generation of the Church—the succession of saints, stretching from the apostolic age to our own day, which Saint Symeon the New Theologian termed the 'golden chain.'*[1]

God has never ceased providing every generation, including our own, with such God-bearing prophet-elders. In Romania, where east and west, monasticism and society, Greek and Slavic Orthodox church tradition have harmoniously converged for the last five centuries, we meet a figure most saintly and unique: the great *staretz* of the Romanian people, the blessed Archimandrite Cleopa Ilie (1912-1998).

He was a rare spiritual personality with the gift to guide souls as well as to instruct the faithful. He was a gifted confessor as well as a beloved Orthodox enlightener and teacher of people from every stratum of society, people who were

1 Ware, Bishop Kallistos, The Spiritual Father in Saint John Climacus and Saint Symeon the New Theologian, foreword to *Spiritual Direction in the Early Christian East* by Irenee Hausherr. Cistercian Press, 1990, pg. vii.

spiritually oppressed by the long decades of communist-atheist rule and tempted by the allure of heterodox creeds like the papal-inspired Uniatism, and the Hungarian and German Protestantism in Transylvania.

The nation-wide appeal of Elder Cleopa had as a pre-condition the manifest "monastic-consciousness" of Romanian society, which itself is derived from the pro-monastic climate of the sixteenth and seventeenth centuries when the Romanian Principalities had many spiritual ties to Mt. Athos, the Holy Land and Mt. Sinai.

It is no coincidence that this modern-day Moses arose out of a monastic-loving family and lived the *hesychia* of the forest monasteries and hermitages of Moldavia from his youth. In the rolling hills and tree-covered mountains of Moldavia, the monk Cleopa travelled into the timeless sphere of Holy Scripture, having the Holy Fathers as his guides and instructors. Following the example of ascetic writers and teachers of ages past—Isidore of Pelusium, St. Nilus the Ascetic, St. John Damascene, St. Theodore the Studite, St. Nicodemos the Athonite and St. Paisius Velichkovsky—he turned the sword of his intellect, sharpened by years of study and contemplation, onto the life-threatening heresies of our day.

His authority derived not from academic titles, but from Holy Scripture and the age-long Orthodox patristic tradition. A confessor and sufferer under the iconoclastic communist regime, the Elder took every opportunity to preach and present an exact exposition of the Orthodox Faith to his contemporaries. A monastery builder and for a time a fugitive cenobiarch, he made *Sihastria,* the monastery of his repentance, into the *Studion* of Romanian monasticism. For almost forty years, thousands of inquiring souls found answers to their questions in front of the monastic ambo of his cell's porch and in his writings and letters. He was relentless in his

Elder Cleopa

struggle to bring relief to the spiritual plight of the faithful who, by necessity and the communist yoke, were deprived of the liberating wisdom of the Holy Fathers. Remaining the spiritual father of practically all the Moldavian monasteries for almost fifty years, Elder Cleopa had a strong desire to see the patristic and hesychast legacy revived in letter and in deed in Romanian monasticism.

He successfully instilled in those who came to him the consciousness of their Orthodox identity and its meaning for their lives. The simple people, the flock of Christ, found in his words an echo of the timeless voice of Holy Tradition. His visage became a national icon of who the Romanians were as

Orthodox Christians, and his words became the lighthouse they needed to transverse the rough seas brought about by the western, materialistic way of life.

The pages that follow—translated accurately into English by Fr. Peter Alban Heers, an American convert and student of Orthodox theology at the Aristotle University of Thessaloniki—record a series of encounters between Elder Cleopa and his Protestant-discipled inquirers.

Unlike most exchanges between Orthodox and Reformed academy-trained theologians, the guidelines of this discussion are clear and the nature of the Church is delineated from the start. Here, you will find no false pretensions as to the presuppositions of the discourse: the Church is One, She is the "pillar and ground of the truth" (1 Tim. 3:15), and She possesses the Apostolic Tradition in its fullness, without which all human attempts at coming to know God fall short. Clarity of thought and freedom of expression enable both seeker and guide to arrive quickly to their desired goal—the Truth: "Ye shall know the truth, and the truth shall make you free" (Jn. 8:32).

May the good-willed seeker approach the venerable counsels of Elder Cleopa in a spirit of discipleship, asking from the Lord eyes of faith and the will to follow Him whatever the cost. And may the pious Orthodox Christian be benefitted and built up in his Faith through the attentive study of the Elder's teachings contained herein.

Archimandrite Joseph
Xeropotamou Monastery, Mount Athos
Holy Great Martyr James the Persian, 11/27/2000

Photograph courtesy of Theodore Doru Vantu. Taken May 1995, Sihastria Monastery, Neamts, Romania

ELDER CLEOPA ILIE OF ROMANIA
1912 - 1998

PROLOGUE

Father Cleopa: The Elder of Romanian Orthodoxy[1]

The name and personality of Elder Cleopa Ilie of Romania is today known not only in his homeland but also throughout the world. Father Cleopa was born in 1912 in the town of Soulitsa and district of Botosani and into a pious village family and named Constantine. His parents were called Alexander and Anna, and he was the ninth of their ten children. The religious upbringing that he and all his siblings received from childhood, as well as their great inclination toward the monastic life, were so strong that five of the ten children, along with their mother in her later years, took up the monastic life and were clothed in the monastic Schema. His spiritual formation was owed, first of all, to the Great-schema hieromonk Father Paisius Olarou of the Kozantsea-Bodosani skete who was for many years the Spiritual Father of his entire family. While spending his childhood years

---

1 This article has been compiled from two different sources: *The Life and Struggles of Elder Cleopa: Romanian Hesychast and Teacher* and *Spiritual Dialogues with Romanian Fathers,* both by Archimandrite Ioanichie Balan in Greek translation. Some excerpts have also been taken from the forthcoming book of the St. Herman Brotherhood, *Shepherd of Souls, Elder Cleopa the New Hesychast of Romania,* also written by Fr. Ioanichie Balan.

shepherding the family's sheep around the forests of Sihastria, the young Constantine, together with his two oldest brothers Basil and George, was being spiritually raised by their spiritual father, hieromonk Paisius.

In the spring of 1929, the three brothers departed their father's house and entered the struggle of the monastic life in the monastery of Sihastria—which, at that time, was under the spiritual direction of Archimandrite Ioannicius Moroi, who was considered one of the greatest and holiest of spiritual fathers in Moldavia. After seven years of trials, the young novice Constantine Ilie was tonsured a monk in 1936 with the name Cleopa and, for a number of years, continued his beloved service of shepherding sheep as the student of a virtuous monk named Fr. Galaction.

For more than ten years, the beloved service in which he was close to the sheep and in the midst of the natural beauty of the mountains and forests of Moldavia was a veritable school of spiritual formation and advancement in humility, stillness, and prayer for Father Cleopa. Surrounded by the majestic Carpathian Mountains, the breeze of silence gently blew across the hillside above the fertile valley of Sihastria, whispering to the aspiring hearts of the young brothers, Basil and Constantine, a reminder of the presence of the Creator. Day flowed into day as time passed imperceptibly. The brothers rarely left the fold and did not even perform the customary cycle of services. Rather, they sought the altar of God within themselves, continually raising their mind's eye to God through the sacred Prayer of the Heart.

It was here at the sheepfold that the soul of the future guide of the Romanian people would be formed. Elder Cleopa would later remember his nostalgic beginnings:

"In the years that I was shepherd of the skete's sheep

together with my brothers, I had great spiritual joy. The sheepfold, the sheep—I lived in quiet and solitude on the mountain, in the midst of nature; it was my monastic and theological school."

"It was then that I read *Dogmatics* by St. John Damascene and his *Precise Exposition of the Orthodox Faith.* How precious this time was to me! When the weather would warm up, we would put the yearling lambs and the rams in Cherry Meadow, which was covered with green grass and surrounded by bushes. They would not stray from there. 'Stay put!' I'd say to them, and then I would read *Dogmatics.*"

"When I would read something about the Most Holy Trinity, the distinctions between angels, man and God, about the qualities of the Most Holy Trinity, or when I read about Paradise and hell—the dogmas about which St. John Damascene wrote—I would forget to eat that day."

"There was an old hut in which I'd take shelter, and there

someone from the skete would bring me food. And when I would return to the hut in the evening, I would ask myself, 'Have I eaten anything today?' All day long I was occupied with reading… When I was with the sheep and cattle I read St. Macarius of Egypt, St. Macarius of Alexandria, and the Lives of the Saints in my knapsack when I first arrived at the monastery. I would read and the day would pass in what seemed like an hour…"

"I would borrow these books from the libraries of Neamts and Secu Monasteries and carry them with me in my knapsack on the mountain. After I had finished my prayer rule, I would take out these books of the Holy Fathers and read them next to the sheep until evening. And it seemed as if I would see Saints Anthony, Macarius the Great, St. John Chrysostom and the others; how they would speak to me. I would see St. Anthony the Great with a big white beard, and, in luminous appearance, he would speak to me so that all he would say to me would remain imprinted on my mind like when one writes on wax with one's finger. Everything that I read then I will never forget…"

In this university of obedience and silence, Father Cleopa read about one hundred theological and miscellaneous works, starting with the theological, moral, liturgical, and hagiographic and ending with the patristic works of the great Saints of our Church, not to mention, of course, the Horologion and Psalter. The most beloved book of all, however, was Holy Scripture. In addition to Scripture, Father Cleopa loved the lives of the Saints, the sayings of the desert fathers, *The Ladder of Divine Ascent* by Saint John Climacus, the ascetical works of Saints Isaac and Ephraim of Syria, as well as the writings of Saints Maximus the Confessor, Gregory Palamas, Symeon the New Theologian and others.

As he was ended with special reverence and much zeal for

the divine, with penetrating insight and comprehension of divine mysteries, and with a powerful memory, in a short amount of time, Father Cleopa was revealed as self-taught and unequalled among the monks of Romanian monasticism. In addition to these gifts of God, he was given the ability to teach and the strength of eloquence. With the beauty of the Moldavian ecclesiastical dialect and the semi-archaic diction of an elder— and by means of preaching from Holy Scripture, selected patristic texts, and instructive ethical stories of all kinds—he presented the Truth to the people of God.

In 1942, although Father Cleopa was still a simple monk, he temporarily assumed the governing of Sihastria in place of the ageing Abbot Ioannicius Moroi who was confined by sickness to his bed. In January of 1945, he was ordained deacon and priest as well as named abbot of Sihastria, serving in this capacity as the shepherd of souls for four years. In this short amount of time, the Elder gathered eighty monks and novices around himself, built new housing inside the walls of the monastery for the monks, erected a winter chapel, restored the monastery to its original cenobitic status, organised it according to the traditional order of hesychastic monastic life, elevated important spiritual fathers, and made many missionary journeys for the salvation of the faithful.

In 1947, the soviets occupied Romania, forcing King Michael to abdicate and immediately followed by the institutionalisation of a communist dictatorship. Monasteries were closed; countless hierarchs, priests, monks, nuns, and other faithful Orthodox were imprisoned, tortured, and murdered.

Thus far, Sihastria had remained untouched in its remote location near the Carpathian Mountains. And although Abbot Cleopa was only thirty-six years old, he had already become a nationally known spiritual leader of the Christian faith. Now that he had been joined by his spiritual father from his youth, Elder Paisius Olaru, and had the support of Fr. Joel Gheorgiu, Sihastria was quickly becoming the spiritual center of Orthodoxy for Romania and therefore a threat to the communist government. By the grace which flowed from the eloquent mouth of Fr. Cleopa, a living faith was imparted to those who had ears to hear. The government now sought to dam the flow of faith by stopping Fr. Cleopa from speaking.

In May of 1948, on the feast of Ss. Constantine and Helen, Father Cleopa delivered a homily in which he said, "May God grant that our own rulers might become as the Holy King and Queen were, that the Church might be able to also commemorate them unto the ages." The next day the state police took him to prison, leaving him in a bedless cell and without bread or water for five days. After being released, Father Cleopa, upon receiving good counsel, fled to the mountains of Sihastria, where he lived in a hut that was mostly underground. There, the elder prayed night and day, seeking the help of God and the Theotokos.

During this time, the elder was visited by the grace of God in the following ways. Fr. Cleopa told his disciples that when he was building his hut, birds would come and sit on his head. Indeed, the first time he served the Liturgy on a stump in front of his hut, as he was communing the Holy Mysteries, a flock of birds came and gathered in a way that he had never seen before. As he gazed upon them in astonishment, he noticed that each bird had the sign of the Cross marked on its forehead.

Another time, after preparing for the Liturgy and reading all the prayers, he set the Antimension on the tree stump and began the Liturgy with the exclamation, "Blessed is

Elder Cleopa: A Shepherd of Souls.

the Kingdom of the Father and of the Son and of the Holy Spirit, now and ever and unto the ages of ages!" Again, the birds appeared and, as they perched on the branch of the tree, began to sing in beautiful and harmonic voices. Fr. Cleopa asked himself, "What could this be?" Immediately, an unseen voice whispered to him, "These are your chanters on the cliros." These signs, as well as others, encouraged the

Elder immensely during his time of exile.

In the summer of 1949, Father Cleopa moved to the monastery of Slatina with thirty monks who were advanced in virtue, intent on renewing the spiritual life there. His interaction with the pious Christians living in the region of northern Moldavia increased his pastoral experience and missionary activity and gave him the opportunity to work with great zeal for the aims of the Gospel of Christ. In particular, his preaching, personal counsel, spiritual direction, compassion, and love spread his renown throughout the country. Through these and other struggles for the salvation of men in Christ, Father Cleopa became the most celebrated and respected Abbot of the monasteries of Romania as well as a spiritual father with pre-eminent spiritual authority. Villager and intellectual, monk and layman, young and old, healthy and sick, bishop and priest—everyone found a true spiritual father in Father Cleopa. He was a model of life for all, who was ready to offer everyone whatever he could, to counsel and give rest, and to lead all to Christ with amazing conviction and authority.

During this time, the Metropolitan of Moldavia asked Father Cleopa to assume the spiritual guidance of most of the monasteries in the region: Putna, Moldovita, Riska, Sihastria, and the Sketes of Sihla and Rareau, according to the prototype of Slatina.

In 1952, Father Cleopa was arrested briefly for a second time by the secret police. Having been released again, he and a monastic brother traveled once more to the mountains of Moldavia until the situation normalized. There in the mountains, the elder battled the demons, lived side by side with wild animals, and prayed night and day, receiving confession and communion from his co-struggling monastic brother.

In 1953, he resigned from the abbacy and, in 1956, after assisting in the re-organisation of the Poutna Monastery and the Raraeu and Gaie sketes, Father Cleopa returned to Sihastria, the monastery of his beloved repentance. Here, he continued his spiritual activity by praying, going deeper into the writings of the Holy Fathers, and guiding his many disciples to spiritual advancement.

From 1959 to 1964, the Church of Romania suffered acute persecution from the Communist regime, with the monasteries undergoing their most difficult days of the twentieth century. In 1959, the government decreed that all monks under the age of fifty-five and all nuns under the age of fifty must leave the monasteries. By the spring of 1960, the state police had removed more than four thousand monastics from Romania's monasteries. Yet again, Father Cleopa was forced into the mountains of Moldavia where he would spend more than twelve hours a day in prayer. It was during this time of exile that the elder wrote several of his well-known guides to the spiritual life for priests and monks. In 1964, the Communist persecutions abated, and the Church experienced a good measure of freedom anew.

In the summer of 1964, to the great joy of all the monks of Sihastria, Father Cleopa returned from the desert and his silence—and, within days, the monastery was filled with pilgrims seeking his counsel and direction. Thus, the apostolic-missionary work of Elder Cleopa began again, delivering soul-benefitting words of instruction to the faithful as well as confessing and directing the pious.

The first duty that Father Cleopa sought from the faithful was the devout preservation of the Orthodox Faith—meaning, all of the dogmas and mysteries of the Holy Orthodox Church—for without true Faith, even if all possible good works are performed, no one can be saved.

Elder Cleopa with the author, Fr. Ioanichie Balan

Secondly, the Elder ascribed great significance to the confession of sins, admonishing the faithful to confess at least four times a year. He taught them: "Brother, when you see that your father or mother is sick, do not call the doctor first, but the priest, for the doctor cannot add to our life even one minute. And if he could lengthen our life, he doesn't do this of himself. Everything rests with God!"

The Elder recommended generally that one should read the Akathist Hymn to the Mother of God together with the morning prayers of the Church, the Supplicatory Canon to the Theotokos in the evening before bed with the oil lamp lit, and the rest of the day to pray the Jesus Prayer as much as possible. However, more than anyone, the Elder prayed for the Church, the faithful, those fallen into great sins, those undergoing the trials and tragedies of life. The prayers of the Elder brought about miraculous results: sicknesses were cured and the ill were returned from the hospital wards healthy; examinations by doctors unexpectedly had positive results; and, generally, the blessings of God were spread everywhere by the prayers of the Elder.

Father Cleopa never tired of encouraging the faithful to give alms and show mercy to others. He would tell them in confession: "Do not turn anyone away from you without showing mercy. If you do not have money to give him, give him potatoes, some bread, a kerchief. Give him something, even a scrap. If you give something, it won't seem hard to you to give something more the next time, for your almsgiving and mercy arises to God like a thunderbolt. Why? Two great virtues are combined: almsgiving and humility."

The primary duty that he asked Christian families to fulfill was the birth and upbringing of children. Following the Holy Canons of the Church, Father Cleopa absolutely condemned the aborting of children and the killing of embryos, one of the greatest sins a Christian could commit.

In 1965, with the exhortation of his disciples and with the blessing of many hierarchs, Father Cleopa began to write homilies, teachings, and soul-benefitting epistles for monastics as well as laymen. Specifically, knowing well the community life of the Romanian people, the misfortunes of the clergy, and (perhaps most of all) the fanatical proselytism of heterodox groups in Romania over the past thirty years, Father Cleopa wrote many apologetic works for the support of the Orthodox Faith and the correction of false teachings. The most important of these works include *Discourse on*

Visions and Dreams—containing seven discussions dealing with the problem of dreams, visions and the question of frequent Holy Communion—and *Heresiology*, a monumental work containing thirty-three dialogues covering the wide range of anti-dogmatic and anti-orthodox teachings of both the heterodox and the faithful but simpleminded. This work was published in 1981 under the title *On the Orthodox Faith*. Other works with moral-instructional character include the following: *Homilies for the Feasts* (1976), containing thirty-six sermons on the Great Feasts of the year; *Homilies for Monks*, a massive work containing forty-eight "philokalian" sermons; *Homilies for the Sundays and Feasts of the Year*, also massive; and *Homilies for Laymen.*

These and other activities constituted the great spiritual missionary work that Elder Cleopa carried out from the Fall of 1964 until the second of December in 1998, which is when he gave his soul into the hands of God. During many of these years, the Elder divided his day into three eight-hour periods. During the first, at night, he rested a little and prayed. During the next period, he read the Holy Fathers and wrote. Finally, during the third period, he gave himself up to his disciples and the pilgrims who came to him from near and far for confession and instruction. In order to be able to pray and write undisturbed, he would leave his nearby cell every morning (only five minutes away from the monastery) and go to one that was located twenty minutes to the north. He would remain there alone for the whole day, writing down adages from his experience, and then he would come down to the cell that was near the monastery in the afternoon to receive the faithful and confess the monks.

Fr. Cleopa—as is the case with every venerable servant of Christ—was, above all, a man of prayer. As a boy, the young Constantine prayed often from books and learned many prayers by heart and continually repeated them. As a youth, he developed a great love for reading the Psalter, which he repeated daily. He also knew by heart the Akathist to the Saviour, the Akathist to the Mother of God, the Canon of Repentance to the Saviour, and the Paraclesis to the Mother of God, all of which he said daily. At the same time, he made three to four hundred prostrations and bows each day.

Under the influence of his ascetically-minded older brothers, Basil and George, he also began to force himself to become accustomed to the Prayer of the Heart, at which the older two became advanced at a young age.

As Abbot of Sihastria Monastery, being very busy during the daytime hours, Fr. Cleopa would pray more at night. He would sleep two hours before Matins and again two more hours after the service, after which he would perform his entire prayer rule for the day, which took three hours. Over the course of the ten years that he spent in the wilderness during his three exiles, he devoted countless hours to the Prayer of the Heart. Even the fingernail with which he would pull the knots of his prayer-rope was deformed because of a lifetime of practicing this prayer.

Fr. Cleopa would speak to his disciples about pure prayer of the heart as if he were speaking of someone else's experience: "I met with someone who had toiled with hunger, with thirst, with cold, with nakedness in the woods and he told me that he had once spent the night in the home of a pious Christian man. On the evening before Sunday, he completed his rule of prayer. At the house of a neighbour, there was a wedding with music. The desert-dweller, being at prayer, had before him an icon of the Mother of God. Standing and pondering, he thought upon the word of St. John of the Ladder, which says: 'Some say songs can raise the advanced to more exalted contemplation.' Thus, hearing the music from the wedding, he said to himself, 'If these people know how to sing so beautifully, how do the angels in heaven sing, who give praise to the Mother of God?' From this feeling, his mind descended into his heart, and he stayed in this prayer for over two hours, feeling much sweetness and warmth. His tears flowed continually, his heart was enflamed and he sensed Christ—how He conversed with his soul. Such a fragrance of the Holy Spirit came upon him then, and he felt so much spiritual warmth, that he said to himself, 'O Lord, I want to die in this moment!'

After two hours, his mind came out from the heart and remained with a sweet sorrow, a joy, a consolation, and an incredible spiritual warmth for a month. The heaven in his heart could no longer be drawn to something from this world, because the tears that stream during such times of prayer, being from the Holy Spirit, wash away all defilement and sinful imaginings and the soul remains pure."

Fr. Cleopa would say of the Prayer of the Heart, "When the mind descends into the heart, then the heart opens up and then it closes. That is, the heart absorbs Jesus, and Jesus absorbs our heart. In that moment, the Bridegroom Christ meets with the bride, that is, our soul!"

For most of Elder Cleopa's life God blessed him with good health. When he reached his seventieth year, however, the Elder began to feel tired and fatigued. The years passed in the mountains, as well as his trials under the Communists, had taken their toll. From 1985 until his repose in 1998 the Elder suffered from illnesses such as a double hernia, kidney stones, a spasmodic right hand, the removal of a cyst, and other sicknesses. All of these trials and illnesses kept the Elder alert and expectant for the arrival of the last hours of his life, always immersed in unceasing prayer and thinking on Christ.

The last twenty years of his life the Elder spent in increased and concentrated prayer: fourteen to fifteen hours a day. He had mystical moments when he did not want to speak to anyone, not even his cell attendant. From four until eight the Elder prayed his morning rule; afterward he confessed monks and lay people until about four in the afternoon, when he began his evening prayer rule, consisting of the Canon of Repentance, canons to the Theotokos, the Supplicatory Canon, Small Compline and other services. At night, the fathers made ready the veranda where the Elder would stand alone in prayer, awe, and wonder at the Creator's majestic handiwork, which he loved very much, at the sheep, and at all of God's creation—until sometime in the midst of the night, when he would rest a bit before beginning again.

During the last months of his life, the Elder could be heard saying often: "Now I am going to my brothers!" and "Leave me to depart to my brothers!" and "I am going to Christ! Pray for me, the sinner."

On the eve of the Elder's departure for the next life, he began to read his morning rule, when his disciple said to him: "Geronda, it's evening now. These prayers should be read tomorrow morning." The Elder answered him, saying "I am reading them now because tomorrow morning I am going to my brothers." On the morning of December 2nd, 1998, at about 2:20 am Elder Cleopa departed for eternity and His Christ.

In the three days that followed his repose before the funeral, thousands of the faithful converged on Sihastria to be close to their Elder one last time in this life. The funeral was attended by huge numbers of the faithful with tears in their eyes upon seeing their Elder leaving them, and yet they were also filled with resurrectional joy and the paschal hymn, "Christ is risen...", on their lips. A great monastic and hesychastic period for the Church of Romania came to an end when Elder Cleopa departed to the place where the just repose, and a golden page was inserted into the history of the Romanian Orthodox Church with its beginning and ending at the hesychastic Monastery of Sihastria in Moldavia.

THE TRUTH
OF OUR FAITH

Fr. Cleopa walking in the cemetery where his
spiritual father, Elder Paisius Olaru, is buried.

INTRODUCTION

By Elder Cleopa

Over the years, the notion of writing this book ripened slowly within me. All sorts of people were passing by my *kelli*[1] for their spiritual needs, requesting a prayer, assistance, and a word of direction. Many more, however, also came with questions regarding the Faith. Some questions were easier and others were harder, depending upon the maturity, the preparation, and the thirst for knowledge that each possessed. A few of these were not only children of the Orthodox Church and well versed in Holy Scripture, but were also world travellers. They had, in the course of their travels, encountered people of other faiths and religious convictions and those who, indeed, were quite modern in their way of thinking. Arriving from the other end of the world, they lacked any relationship with our Orthodox Church or the roots of our Romanian nation.

With these people, I had conversations (occasionally lengthy and laborious) about the faith. I was ever hastening

---

1 The *kelli* (κελλί) of a monk is known in English as his "cell," the room or house in which he lives out his ascetic struggle.

to Holy Scripture and the Holy Fathers in search of their deeper, internal meaning. Our discussions together set these people thinking. They asked if that which they had received from their parents and ancestors with regard to religious faith is actually representative of the truth of Holy Revelation. Sometimes they came with Holy Scripture in hand and questions written. Other times they were carrying the answers that their teachers had given them.

I never scolded any believer for having doubts about the Faith, nor did I ask anyone to believe blindly. If I had done so, this would have meant that I was forcing them to accept the Orthodox Faith, not unlike those who ask them to believe their own faith without allowing them to make even one inquiry. On the contrary, I considered it imperative that these discussions be offered as valuable indications to the inquirer of my sole desire for him to know the truth of our Orthodox Faith. I was not disappointed. I had the joy of seeing the fruit of such discussions in those who had come with troubled faith. Afterward, they departed with tranquillity and clarity of thought, like a mountain spring.

Then, I began to think: there will be many others still who, with minds harassed by various questions, would not be able to obtain answers. Furthermore, who would help them if not the priest of their parish? Yet, do they all have the same measure of spiritual age and pastoral ability? Of course not. For this reason, in spite of my limited spiritual strength, I decided to write this book. May it yield some benefit to my brethren! At first, I classified the material in chapters according to the testimony of our Faith. Afterward, I attended to their meaning in order to make the book more comprehensible by using as a framework this dialogue of orthodox priest and inquirer—a soul thirsting to arrive at the knowledge of

the truth of our Faith, yet carrying questions, internal un-
certainty, and, at times, being swayed by the outside world.

Archimandrite Cleopa Ilie
Feast of the Ascension of the Lord
The Holy Monastery of Sihastria, Romania
1980

The Synaxis of the Twelve Apostles

Portable Icon from the Catholicon of the Holy Monastery of Karakalou, Mount Athos. Work of Hieromonk Dionysios of Fourna, 1722.

CHAPTER 1

On the Church

ELDER CLEOPA: For what reason, my child, would you like to speak with me?

INQUIRER: I want the truth of the Faith made known to me.

EC: Yes, it is good for us to seek the truth about everything. Yet, what would you like to ask first of all?

INQ.: To begin with, tell me, what is "the Church"?

EC: "The Church" is the holy foundation that has been laid by the Incarnate Word of God for the salvation and sanctification of man.

INQ.: I would like to learn how you understand the meaning of "The Church" in Holy Scripture.

EC: The word "Church" in Holy Scripture has many meanings and names. It is used sometimes with one meaning, other times with another, sometimes with one name, other times with another.

Inq.: What are these various meanings and names of the Church in Holy Scripture?

EC: To begin with, in the New Testament, the word Church means the highest level of the hierarchy and leadership of the Church, through which Christ laid the foundation in a particular place by the fullness of Orthodox Christian Baptism in the Name of the Holy Trinity.

Inq.: What is this "supreme hierarchy" that was inaugurated in the Church by Christ the Saviour?

Mat. 18:18
Heb. 13:17
Acts 20:28
Jn. 20:22-23

EC: It was set up by the Holy Apostles and their successors to consist of bishops, priests, and deacons.

Inq.: When did the Saviour establish it in the Church?

Lk. 10:16
Jn. 20:21

EC: When He said to His Apostles: "He that heareth you heareth Me; and he that despiseth you despiseth Me; and he that despiseth Me, despiseth Him that sent Me," and "As My Father hath sent Me, even so I send you."

Inq.: What exceptional powers did the Saviour give to this hierarchy?

Jn. 20:22-23
Mat. 18:18

1 Cor. 5:4-5
1 Tim. 1:20
Mat. 16:18-19

Acts 2:1-12

EC: First of all, He gave to His disciples the power to bind and loose the sins of man in heaven and on earth. He gave them the power of discipline in the Church in order to chastise those transgressing the commandments of Christ. He clothed them with power from on high with the descent of the Holy Spirit. He sent them to preach the Gospel to all the world and to baptize their disciples in the Name of the Holy Trinity, "of the Father, and of the Son, and of the Holy Spirit."

Mat. 28:18-20

INQ.: Is this conception of the Church correct?

EC: Yes. The conception of the Church, as seen in Holy Scripture, is composed of those Christians who, following the Holy Apostles, were baptised by them in the Name of the Holy Trinity.

Mat. 16:18

Col. 1:18-20

INQ.: Which passages of Holy Scripture testify to this understanding of the Church?

EC: The Church—the sum total of true, faithful Christians, shepherd and flock, in one place—has ample testimony in that which pertains to her: "For as we have many members in one body, and all members have not the same office, so we, being many, are one body in Christ, and every one members one of another." The body is the Church, while Christ is Her Head.

Rom. 12:4-5

Col. 1:18-24

INQ.: How is the word "Church" interpreted in Holy Scripture?

EC: In addition to the foregoing, we understand the word "Church" in Holy Scripture to mean the church building, that is, the place of worship.

INQ.: How is the Church understood as a place of worship?

EC: We understand the Church as the holy place designed and intended for collective or public worship just as was the temple in the Old Testament. With this meaning, we encounter the Church in many places of Holy Scripture. The Saviour, still a child, honoured the holy place as the true place of worship when, at the age of twelve, He came with His parents to worship in the church. As a place of worship, the Saviour named it "My House," and every day He was found in it teaching the people. We find it with the same meaning in the work of the Holy Apostles. Coming to Antioch, the Apostles Paul and Barnabas "assembled themselves in[1] the church and taught much people." Similarly, Paul also referred to this meaning, saying, "As in all the churches of the saints (of the Christians), the women should keep silence in the churches." In this passage, the meaning of the word "church" is plain and is manifest as a place of assembly for the common worship.

INQ.: How many other names are ascribed to the Church in Holy Scripture?

EC: It is called: God's husbandry[a], the Bride of Christ[b], the church of the saints[c], council of the upright[d], church of the firstborn[e], one flock of Christ[f], golden lampstands[g], city of God[h], city of the Living God[i], the pillar and ground of the truth[j], the congregation of the saints[k], the body of Christ[l], God's building[m], a glorious church[n], Bride of the Lamb[o], family of God in heaven and earth[p], House of the God of Jacob[q], House of Christ[r], New Jerusalem[s] and other names.

INQ.: Which Church do we Christians have?

EC: The Church of Christ is one because she was founded

Luke 2:46-48
Mat. 21:13
Jn. 18:20
Acts 11:26
1 Cor. 14:34

a 1 Cor. 3:9
b 2 Cor. 11:2
c Ps. 149:1
d Psalm 110:1
e Heb. 12:23
f Jn. 10:16
g Rev. 1:20
h Psalm 86:2
i Rev. 21:2
j 1 Tim. 3:15
k Psalm 88:5
l Eph. 1:22-23
m 1 Cor. 3:9
n Eph. 5:27
o Rev. 19:7
p Eph. 3:15
q Is. 2:2-3
r Heb. 3:6
s Rev. 3:12

---

1 While the KJV has rendered the Greek "with the Church," the original text actually reads "*in* the Church" (ἐν τῇ ἐκκλησίᾳ).

a Mat. 16:18

b Eph. 5:27

c Heb. 3:6

d Rom. 12:5

e Jn. 10:16

by the one and only Saviour[a]. One is her Head, even Jesus Christ, and she is imaged forth as His bride[b], as a house of God and of Christ[c], as the sole body of Christ[d], as the one unique flock[e]. She is called holy because her Head is holy and in her dwells the Holy Spirit.

INQ.: When sinners dwell in the Church, how is it possible for it to remain holy?

James 3:2

1 Tim. 1:15

Mat. 13:24-30

Mat. 13:47-50

2 Tim. 2:20

Mat. 9:12

EC: Sinners do not taint the holiness of the Church. Her mission is exactly this: to extend sanctification to sinners. All men are sinners and no one can say that he is without sin. Some heterodox allege that only holy people are assembled in their community. However, they suppose falsely, since even the vessel of election himself, the Apostle Paul, says that he is the worst of sinners. The Saviour likens His Church to the parables of the field containing the wheat and the tares and the net that catches both good and worthless fish. St. Paul says that the Church is a house in which are found vessels cast for honourable use and others for dishonourable use. The Saviour did not come to call the righteous but sinners to repentance, because "they that are whole need not a physician, but they that are sick."

The *Nicene Symbol of Faith*

INQ.: Why do the Orthodox say that their Church is "Catholic" and "Apostolic?"

EC: With the word "Catholic" we may suggest that the Church has it as Her purpose to spread throughout the whole world, comprising Christians of every place, of every age, and of all people. This is confirmed by the following commandment of Christ: "Go ye therefore, and teach all

Mat. 28:19

nations . . ." Moreover, the Church is called Catholic since its *entire* teaching is the undistorted truth, which was given by Christ to the Apostles and through them to the world. On the contrary, heresy possesses but a portion of the truth. Orthodoxy is not only the right faith but also the *fullness* of the faith, which is why it is also understood to be synodical[2]. The Church is called "Apostolic" because Christ founded Her through the Apostles, and the Apostles ordered and organised Her. The teaching of Christ is maintained unadulterated through the Apostles. The gifts of the Holy Spirit rest upon the Apostles and through the surety and consistency of apostolic grace and succession are, even today, preserved in the Church. We also say Apostolic because Christ, the chief cornerstone, established the Church upon the spiritual foundation of the Apostles. The Church lives life in Christ, as directed by the Apostles, who are the foremost scribes of

Eph. 2:20

Bible, Church, Tradition: An Eastern Orthodox View, pp. 41-43

Saint Cyril of Jerusalem

Acts 4:32
Jn. 17:23

2 Elder Cleopa is speaking here of the Church's wholeness or catholicity. Father George Florovsky explains it in this way: "The catholicity of the Church is not a quantitative or a geographical conception. It does not at all depend on the world-wide dispersion of the faithful. The universality of the Church is the consequence or the manifestation, but not the cause or the foundation of its catholicity. . . . The Church was catholic even when the Christian communities were but solitary rare islands in a sea of unbelief and paganism. And the Church will remain catholic even unto the end of time when the mystery of the "falling away" will be revealed, when the Church once more will dwindle to a "small flock" . . . καθολικὴ from καθ᾽ ὅλου means, first of all, the inner wholeness and integrity of the Church's life. . . . If the Church also means universality, it certainly is not an empirical universality, but an ideal one; the communion of ideas, not of facts, is what it has in view. The first Christians when using the words Ἐκκλησία Καθολικὴ (Church Catholic) never meant a world-wide Church. This word rather gave prominence to the orthodoxy of the Church, to the truth of the 'Great Church,' as contrasted with the spirit of sectarian separatism and particularism; it was the idea of integrity and purity that was expressed. . . . The Church is called catholic, because . . . in the Church the dogmas are taught 'fully, without any omission, catholically and completely'. . . . The Church is catholic, because it is the one Body of Christ; it is union in Christ, oneness in the Holy Ghost — and this unity is the highest wholeness and fulness. The gauge of catholic union is that 'the multitude of them that believed be of one heart and of one soul' . . . The growth of the Church is in the perfecting of its inner wholeness, its inner catholicity, in the 'perfection of wholeness'; 'that they may be made perfect in one.'"

the words of the Saviour.

INQ.: What do we Orthodox mean when we say that we have two churches—one in heaven, victorious, and one on earth, still contending?

EC: We do not say that we have two churches, but only one. However, we do recognize that it is spread within two realms: in the visible of the living and the invisible of the reposed. The visible is also called the militant or contesting because its members are still found struggling with the powers of the wicked adversary. The unseen is called triumphant or victorious since its members have defeated the powers of the adversary and have gone over to the heavenly world together with the Angels. Hence, our Church—which is one—has both those living on the earth and those reposed in the heavens, glorifying God and praying for the salvation of the entire world.

Eph. 6:11-13
Gal. 5:17

Heb. 12:23
Eph. 5:27

ⲞⲘⲀⲢⲔⲞⳞ

Mark the Evangelist

CHAPTER 2

On Holy Scripture

INQUIRER: What do we mean by the term "Holy Scripture?"

ELDER CLEOPA: The term Holy Scripture denotes the sum of holy books that were written under the inspiration of the Holy Spirit within a time period of close to 1,500 years, namely, from Moses, 1,400 years before Christ, until the writer of the Apocalypse, nearly 100 years after Christ.

INQ.: Why don't the bishops and priests sanction Christians, who are members of the Church, to interpret and preach publicly the word of God from the Scriptures?

EC: Each Christian has the need to read Holy Scripture, yet each Christian does not also have the authority or ability to teach and interpret the words of Scripture. This privileged authority is reserved for the Church via its holy clergy and theologians, men who are instructed in and knowledgeable of the true faith. When we consider how our Saviour gave the grace of teaching to His Holy Apostles and not to the masses;

Mat. 28:20

it is easy for us to see that the prerogative to teach is held only by the bishops, priests and theologians of our Church. It was the Apostles who were sent by Christ to teach and to celebrate the Holy Mysteries (Sacraments). Our Apostle Paul says: "How shall they preach, except they be sent?" Accordingly, the bishops are the lawful successors to the Apostles and those sent for the preaching (κήρυγμα) to the people. Paul entrusts the heavy burden of the instruction of the people to Timothy and not to the faithful. He speaks of this elsewhere: "Are all apostles? Are all prophets? Are all teachers?" Again he says to Timothy that the clergy must be "apt to teach" others. He does not, however, say the same thing for the faithful. He makes a distinction between shepherd and sheep, between teacher and those taught. Still, the teachers cannot teach whatever they would like, but that which the Church teaches universally. They teach in the name of the Church and of Christ. Not everyone has the intellectual ability and the requisite divine grace necessary to expound Holy Scripture correctly. The Apostle Peter also says this in his second epistle, referring to the epistles of the Apostle Paul. He says the following: "There are some things in them hard to understand, which the ignorant and unstable twist to their own destruction, as they do the other scriptures."

Inq.: Some say that it is not right that members of the Church don't have the right to interpret and expound upon Scripture. As this excerpt says, each Christian knows how to render Holy Scripture: "But ye have an unction from the Holy One, and ye know all things," and "the anointing which ye have received of him abideth in you, and ye need not that any man teach you."

Rom. 10:15

1 Cor. 12:29

1 Tim. 3:2

2 Peter 3:16

1 John 2:20,27

EC: Holy Scripture is like a very deep well wherein is comprised the infinite wisdom of God. If someone thirsty dives into this well to drink of all its water, he will be drowned within. If, however, he will fetch the water with a bucket and from there will drink with a cup, then there is no fear of being engulfed. What man is so crazed as to wish to plunge into such an abyss of water without knowing how to swim? Holy Scripture, according to the Fathers, is "bone" and no one will venture with teeth "fit for milk" to break the strong bones of Holy Scripture – for those teeth will be crushed.

You've read in Scripture about the eunuch of Candace, Queen of the Ethiopians? He was reading the Prophet Isaiah when the Apostle Philip asked him if he understood that which he read, to which he replied: "How can I, except some man should guide me?"

Acts 8:31

You realize also that the word "unction," or "anointing" (χρῖσμα) that you mentioned above means the effusion of the Holy Spirit in the Mystery of Holy Chrism, directly after Baptism.

Acts 8:17

The phrase "you know all things" signifies everything that contains Christian truth and salvation, as well as everything that is related to the antichrist and his adherents, to whom the subsequent verse of the epistle of the holy John the Theologian refers. One must not, therefore, teach according to one's own understanding and perception, for one will be deceived.

INQ.: All the same, it is said that each Christian has the right and obligation to read Holy Scripture on his own, as the Saviour admonishes us: "You search the Scriptures, because you think that in them you have eternal life; and it is they that bear witness of me."

Jn. 5:39

EC: Be careful, because many heretics of earlier eras made bold to immerse themselves in the fathomless sea of Scripture and drowned spiritually, thus perishing together with as many as followed them. They don't have all the same spiritual maturity. They are not all able to understand the mystery of Holy Scripture.

Holy Scripture is understood and explained in three ways: 1) according to its literal meaning, namely the nominal, grammatical, verbal and historical, 2) allegorically or metaphorically, which is superior to the former, and 3) spiritually. According to the Fathers, the simplest of senses to alight upon is the first meaning, according to the letter of Scripture; to penetrate with discretion to the nature of Scripture requires modest learning, while to explain the depth of the meanings of Scripture is of the highest spiritual advancement and in need of the most divine grace. The perfect wisdom of Scripture belongs, according to Saint Paul, to the perfect: "Howbeit we speak wisdom among them that are perfect: yet not the wisdom of this world, nor of the princes of this world, that come to naught: But we speak the wisdom of God in a mystery, even the hidden wisdom, which God ordained before the world unto our glory."

1 Cor. 2:6-7

INQ.: There are those who contend that it is not necessary for someone to have much learning to be able to understand the teachings of Scripture, since to the unlearned He revealed the wisdom of these teachings, just as the Saviour says: "I thank Thee, O Father, . . . because Thou hast hid these things from the wise and prudent, and hast revealed them unto babes."

Mat. 11:25

EC: Yes, God revealed His wisdom to those that were known to be babes in wickedness but not in mind[1] and judgement. In other words, He revealed His wisdom to those who, with respect to good works, were perfect and had attained to the innocence of infants. That's why Paul counsels the Corinthians as follows: "Brethren, be not children in understanding: howbeit in malice be ye children, but in understanding be ye men."

1 Cor. 14:20

INQ.: Yet, God rebuked the wisdom and knowledge of men, as this passage indicates: "I will destroy the wisdom of the wise, and will bring to nothing the understanding of the prudent." Saint Paul also says: "Where is the wise? Where is the scribe? Where is the disputer of this world? Hath not God made foolish the wisdom of this world?" Might it not be that God is not able to give the wisdom of understanding the Scriptures to certain people who are worldly-wise, as the Orthodox maintain?

Is. 29:14

1 Cor. 1:19

EC: You should know that God does not condemn just any wisdom and knowledge, but that which kills man spiritually. If He were to censure every wisdom, He would have to reject also the wisdom of Solomon, the wisdom of Joshua, son of Sirac, the wisdom of Christ the Saviour, and the wisdom of the Prophets and Apostles, to whom He gave the command-

---

1 νοῦς, νοός, νοΐ, νοῦν mind, thought, reason; attitude, intention, purpose; understanding, discernment: The English word that best conveys the meaning of the Greek word νοῦς is probably the word "mind", however, it also has other meanings as well. The Fathers refer to the *nous* as the "soul" (the "spiritual nature" of a man, St. Isaac the Syrian) and the "heart" (or the "essence of the soul"). More particularly, it constitutes the innermost aspect of the heart (St. Diadochos). Yet, it is also referred to as the "eye of the soul" (St. John of Damascus) or the "organ of theoria" (St. Macarius of Egypt) which is "engaged in pure prayer" (St. Isaac the Syrian). In this book the words "mind" and "intellect" have been used most often when rendering the Greek word νοῦς.

Mat. 10:16

ment to be "wise as serpents, and harmless as doves." Yet, it isn't like this in the least. Hence, take care not to resemble those to whom the Saviour said: "You do err, not knowing the Scriptures, nor the power of God."

Mat. 22:29

INQ.: Is Holy Scripture sufficient in order to guide man to salvation?

EC: No, it is not sufficient to guide man to salvation,[2] inasmuch as, firstly, it wasn't given to man from the beginning and, secondly, when it was given it wasn't the only authentic text, with regard to the salvation of human souls, because before it there was the Holy Tradition. Many years before Moses began writing the first books of the Old Testament, there was sacred piety in the community of the people of Israel. Similarly, the books of the New Testament began to be written ten years after the formal foundation of the Church, which took place on the day of Pentecost. The Church chose and sealed as inspired by God the books of the two

Fr. George
Florovsky
*Bible, Church,
Tradition:
An Eastern
Orthodox View,*
pp. 48–49

2 "We cannot assert that Scripture is self-sufficient; and this is not because it is incomplete, or inexact, or has any defects, but because Scripture in its very essence does not lay claim to self-sufficiency. . . . If we declare Scripture to be self-sufficient, we only expose it to subjective, arbitrary interpretation, thus cutting it away from its sacred source. Scripture is given to us in tradition. It is the vital, crystallising centre. The Church, as the Body of Christ, stands mystically first and is fuller than Scripture. This does not limit Scripture, or cast shadows on it. But truth is revealed to us not only historically. Christ appeared and still appears before us not only in the Scriptures; He unchangeably and unceasingly reveals Himself in the Church, in His own Body. In the times of the early Christians the Gospels were not yet written and could not be the sole source of knowledge. The Church acted according to the spirit of the Gospel, and, what is more, the Gospel came to life in the Church, in the Holy Eucharist. In the Christ of the Holy Eucharist, Christians learned to know the Christ of the Gospels, and so His image became vivid to them."

1 Tim. 3:15

Testaments over one hundred years later[3]. These then comprised the declared Canon of the books of Holy Scripture. Thereafter the Church maintained this Canon of Truth, inasmuch as it is the very "pillar and ground of truth." The Holy Spirit operates within all of this for the preservation of the truth about salvation. Where the Church is, says Saint Jerome, there also is the Spirit of God and where the Spirit of God is, there also is the Church and all grace – since the Spirit is truth.

St. John the Theologian

Icon by Photios Kontoglou

Fr. Alexander Schmemann

The Historical Road of Eastern Orthodoxy,

pg. 44

3 By the end of the first century . . . the Church possessed the four Gospels of Matthew, Mark, Luke, and John. Although they were not perhaps as yet collected into one volume, each had been accepted by the group of churches for which it was written. Very soon afterward they were combined in one quadripartite Gospel, and in the middle of the second century the Christian apologist Tatian composed the first harmony, or code, of the Gospels. . . The appearance of the New Testament in the Church as a book, as Scripture, was therefore not a new factor, but a record of the founding tradition. Just because it *was* identical with the original tradition as the Church already knew it, there appeared at first no need of a canon, or precisely fixed list of accepted records of Scripture." In fact, for the western Church, it was not until 419 AD at the Council of the 217 blessed Fathers assembled at Catharge that the entire New Testament as we know it today was irrevocably canonised (Canon XXIV). – Editor

Christ the Vine with the Apostles

I am the vine, ye are the branches: He that abideth in me, and I in him, the same bringeth forth much fruit: for without me ye can do nothing. . . If ye abide in me, and my words abide in you, ye shall ask what ye will, and it shall be done unto you (Jn. 15: 1-8).

CHAPTER 3

On Holy Tradition

INQUIRER: What is the Holy Tradition that the Orthodox consider to be the second source of Holy Revelation and coequal with Holy Scripture?

ELDER CLEOPA: Holy Tradition is the teaching of the Church, God-given with a *living voice*, from which a portion was later written down. As with Holy Scripture, so too Holy Tradition contains Holy Revelation, and is, therefore, fundamental for our salvation. Holy Tradition is *the life of the Church in the Holy Spirit* and, consonant with the enduring life of the Church, is thus a wellspring of Holy Revelation such that, consequently, it possesses the same authority as Holy Scripture.

From the time of Adam until that of Abraham, according to the old chronologies, 3,678 years passed, and if we add 430 years when the Israelites remained in Egypt, we have 4,108 years. Throughout this period of time, neither did Holy Scripture exist nor was the Sabbath considered as a feast among the people. During this period of many thousands of years, the faithful and chosen people were guided to the path of salvation only by Holy Tradition, namely, from the teachings about God which they received from a living voice. Only for the duration of 1400 years—from the time of Moses until the advent of Christ—were they guided by the Holy Scriptures of the Old Testament.

Just as before the books of the [early Old Testament] people of God were guided in the knowledge of God and on the path of salvation only by Holy Tradition, so too were they guided in precisely the same manner before the writing of the books of the New Testament. The Holy Tradition was the guide by which the first Christians were directed to the path of salvation. The first to impart the teachings of the New Testament with a living voice to the ears of the people was our Saviour Jesus Christ Himself, who for three and a half years continually taught the people, distributing His Gospel without, however, writing anything. Inasmuch as He was carrying out obedience to His Father, He did not send His Apostles to write but to preach the Gospel to the whole world, saying to them: "Go ye therefore, and teach all nations, baptizing them in the name of the Father, and of the Son, and of the Holy Spirit: Teaching them to observe all things whatsoever I have commanded you: and lo, I am with you always, even unto the end of the world. Amen." From the day of its establishment (33 AD) until the year 44 AD, when the Holy Apostle Matthew wrote the first Gospel[1], the Church was governed without the Scriptures of the New Testament, but only with the Holy Tradition of which only a part was later recorded. Although there were many other writers for whom it was claimed that they were inspired and faithful scribes of the Apostles, the Church is She who did or

Mat. 28:19-20

J. Karabido-poulos, Intro. to the N.T., p. 104 (Greek)

1 There are scholars who believe that, in fact, "the writing of the three first Gospels is placed. . . around the year 70 AD."

did not recognise them, for She is unerring. The Church lived the truth of the Gospel even before anything was committed to writing, having lived with the Holy Tradition from the outset.

So then, this is the Holy Tradition: The source and the root of the two Testaments—the Old and the New—and thus the reason why we call it a source of Holy Revelation, since it carries the same weight as Holy Scripture.

INQ.: Yes, but it is said that Holy Scripture as God's word is not permitted to be substituted or exchanged with Tradition, which is man's word, as is written in the Gospel: "Why do you also transgress the commandment of God by your tradition? . . . ye made the commandment of God of none effect by your tradition. Ye hypocrites, well did Isaiah prophesy of you, saying: 'This people . . . in vain do they worship me, teaching for doctrine the commandments of men." Thus, it is not necessary for us to replace or add the tradition of men to the law of God, which is contained in Holy Scripture.

Mat. 15:3, 6-9
Mk. 7:13

EC: What your friends have told you is not at all true, since the law of God is not only contained in Holy Scripture. Listen to what the divine Evangelist John says: "And there are also many other things which Jesus did, the which, if they should be written every one, I suppose that even the world itself could not contain the books that should be written. Amen." Again, the same Evangelist declares in one of his epistles: "Having many things to write unto you, I would not write with paper and ink: but I trust to come unto you, and speak face to face, that our joy may be full." So, you see that the holy Evangelist, when he had the ability, taught his disciples more with the living voice of Tradition than by sending them epistles. While your friends keep at all costs

Jn. 21:25

2 Jn. 1:12

only so much as is written, they do not take into account that both the Saviour and the majority of His Apostles did not leave anything written, but rather taught orally, with the living voice of Tradition.

INQ.: In that case, I do not know how Christians are to understand the statement that we must not be seduced by the false teachings of men, especially those which are religious and rely on Scripture. After all, the Apostle counsels us: "Beware lest any man spoil you through philosophy and vain deceit, after the tradition of men, after the rudiments of the world, and not after Christ." It is our responsibility, then, to preserve ourselves from the false traditions of men.

Col. 2:8

EC: Dearest to Christ, you do not discern the difference between the teachings of human traditions and those that proceed from the apostolic and evangelical tradition. You brought here an excerpt from Holy Scripture that refers to the tradition of human teachings and pseudo-philosophy that has no relationship whatsoever to the evangelical and apostolic Tradition of the Church of Jesus Christ. Holy Tradition is neither a tradition of men, nor a philosophy, nor some kind of trickery, but is the word of God that He delivered to us personally. The great Apostle Paul teaches and exhorts us to keep with vigour the traditions, saying; "Therefore, brethren, stand fast, and hold the traditions which ye have been taught, whether by word, or our epistle." On the contrary, some counsel weaker Christians to slander and abandon the apostolic and evangelical traditions, without understanding that Holy Scripture itself is a fruit of the Holy Spirit that grew out of the roots and tree of Holy Tradition.

2 Thess. 2:15

INQ.: Why is Holy Scripture not sufficient for faith and

salvation without having any need whatsoever of Tradition? This appears to be the case from the words of the Apostle Paul to Timothy: "And that from a child thou hast known the holy Scriptures, which are able to make thee wise unto salvation through faith which is in Christ Jesus. All Scripture is given by inspiration of God, and is profitable for doctrine, for reproof, for correction, for instruction in righteousness." These words are clear. Any addition to Holy Scripture is unnecessary.

2 Tim. 3:15-16

EC: Here, he is speaking only about the Scripture of the Old Testament, for the New Testament had not yet been written. Paul wrote to Timothy that a good teacher could use the Old Testament for the support of his faith in Christ and his instruction in Christianity. According to the notion that you mistakenly asserted, it follows that not one book of the New Testament—from those that were written in the period that followed these epistles of the Apostle Paul to Timothy—should be accepted. Rather, it is enough for us to recognize the Old Testament books mentioned here in the passage to which you refer.

INQ.: Some people do not acknowledge the Tradition because they say that with the passing of time it yielded to many illegitimate elements so that, especially today, we are no longer able to discern the true apostolic Tradition from the false.

EC: The Church of Christ determined the truths of the faith, according to the long course of Tradition, through the teachings and canons of the holy Ecumenical Councils, decrees and the Symbol of Faith [The Creed], and with confessions [of Faith] by holy and wonderworking hierarchs such as were made at the many local synods which have been held continuously since the days of old. At these synods, the authenticity and genuineness of the holy Orthodox Faith was firmly established, primarily therein where it was attacked by the existing heresies of the time. From the totality of such synods appears the irrevocable and inalterable content of Holy Tradition. This is understood when you examine closely the essence of the following conditions:

- Do not sanction conceptions that contain inconsistencies amongst themselves or contradictions with the apostolic Tradition and Holy Scripture. (A teaching is to be considered worthy of "Tradition" when it stems from the Saviour or the Holy Apostles and is directly under the influence of the Holy Spirit.)

- The Tradition is that which has been safeguarded by and derived from the Apostolic Church and has an uninterrupted continuity until today.

- The Tradition is that which is confessed and practiced by the entire universal Orthodox Church.

- The Tradition is that which is in harmony with the greatest portion of the fathers and ecclesiastical writers.

When a tradition does not fulfil these stipulations, it cannot be considered true and holy, and consequently cannot be considered admissible or fit to be observed.

INQ.: Notwithstanding all the efforts which you say the Orthodox Church has made and makes relative to the truth of Tradition, some believe only the teachings which are contained in Holy Scripture. For the first Christians—they say—accepted only such writings as were contained in Holy Scripture, as it is written: "These were more noble than those in Thessalonica, in that they received the word with all

Acts 17:11

readiness of mind and searched the Scriptures daily, whether those things were so." From this, it follows that we should keep those teachings found written in Holy Scripture.

EC: However, the great Apostle Paul commends the Christians of Corinth not because they kept the written teachings, but because they obeyed him and observed with diligence the oral teachings that they had received from him. Listen to what he writes: "Now I praise you, brethren, that ye remember me in all things, and even as I delivered to you, ye are holding fast the traditions." I wonder, what is better to do: for us to keep only the written teachings or to follow the great Apostle Paul who extols those who keep the unwritten tradition as well? Furthermore, we have established that the Holy Apostles and Evangelists believed and preached abundantly from Holy Tradition, which they inherited from of old and which is not written anywhere in Holy Scripture.

1 Cor. 11:2

INQ.: Where, specifically, does it appear that the Holy Apostles taught other teachings aside from those which are written in Holy Scripture?

EC: Here are two testimonies: The Holy Apostle Jude in his catholic epistle, verse nine, among others, says: "But when the archangel Michael, contending with the devil, disputed about the body of Moses, he did not presume to pronounce a reviling judgement upon him, but said, The Lord rebuke thee." Dearest to Christ, search all of Holy Scripture and see if you will find written this utterance. Still further down in the same epistle the Apostle refers to the prophecy of Enoch, saying: "And Enoch also, the seventh from Adam, prophesied of these, saying, Behold, the Lord cometh with ten thousand of his saints, to execute judgement upon all, and to convince

Jude 9

all that are ungodly among them of all their ungodly deeds which they have committed in such an ungodly way, and of all their hard speeches which ungodly sinners have spoken against him." Yet, the Apostle Jude is not alone in speaking from Tradition. Listen to what the illustrious Paul says in his second epistle to Timothy; "Now as Jannes and Jambres withstood Moses, so do these also resist the truth: men of corrupt minds, reprobate concerning the faith." And again, the renowned Apostle Paul, guiding the priests of Ephesus, says: "Remember the words of the Lord Jesus, how he said, it is more blessed to give than to receive." Now, I ask you, who insist on putting faith only in the written word, from where did the two Apostles—Jude and Paul—take the foregoing words, for you will not find them written anywhere in Holy Scripture?

INQ.: Still, I question if it is possible for Holy Tradition to be preserved until today unadulterated and genuine in all respects as in the beginning. Should we not possess more assurances from the written teachings of Holy Scripture?

EC: You saw above that the famed Paul commends the Christians of Corinth for keeping, with care and mindfulness, the unwritten traditions, such as they had received from his very lips. Moreover, you heard that the Apostles Paul and Jude employed in their preaching words taken directly from Holy Tradition such as those that referred to the prophecy of Enoch and others. Further, I also pointed out to you by what means Holy Tradition was preserved throughout the ages. Furthermore, the same Apostle Paul exhorts and directs the Christians of Thessalonica to be very attentive and vigilant to keep the Holy Tradition: "Therefore, brethren, stand fast, and hold the traditions which ye have been taught, whether

Jude 14-20

2 Tim. 3:8

Acts 20:35

2 Thess. 2:15   by word, or our epistle." And in another place, he says: "But though we, or an angel from heaven, preach any other gospel unto you than that which we have preached unto you, let him

Gal. 1:8   be accursed." In other words, he is speaking of the Gospel that he handed down to them with a living voice and not only by written word.

INQ.: How was this Canon of Holy Tradition in the Church preserved over the span of thousands of years? In our age, some allege that from day to day the clergy and ecclesiastical writers alter the truth of Holy Scripture and the Apostolic Tradition, which in the beginning was authentic and genuine. They say that if you have in your hand a book that was published 50 years ago and you put it next to one published recently, they would have nothing in common. It follows, then, that if the hierarchs and priests have done this with the sacred books, they would do the same with the Holy Tradition of which the Orthodox boast as having preserved unscathed from the Holy Apostles.

Mat. 10:17-20
John 4:16-26
1 Tim. 3:15

Mat. 28:20

EC: That which your companions have accepted is not at all correct. The teachings of the Church of Christ are safeguarded by the Holy Spirit and cannot err. Its very founder, Jesus Christ governs it in an unseen way, until the end of the ages. If some ecclesiastical writers, hierarchs, priests or laity translated the Bible from another language or amended some passage of which an expression does not correspond to the present-day speech of our people, this would be an adjustment and modification of expression and not a serious alteration of the substance of the Biblical text. If today a Romanian from the time of the Elder Mirtsea or Stephan the Great (1504) were resurrected and you wanted to speak with him, you would understand him with difficulty, the language having developed, no longer being exactly that which was spoken then. That is exactly what happened regarding the books. With the passage of time the writers' words or expressions were amended with suitable present-day language without, however, changing the meaning of the profound and sacred writings. Previously, I referred you to the foundation upon which Holy Tradition rests and by what means the preservation of its authentic original image is ensured and is conveyed through the ages. This refers to, namely, the ancient Symbol of Faith (The Creed), the apostolic canons and the dogmatic decisions of the seven[2] Ecumenical Councils. To these can also be added the following monumental and meaningful testaments—assurances of the unimpaired preservation of the Holy Tradition:

+104 AD

+106 AD

Eusebius of Caesarea, Ecclesiastical History, Bk 2:36

- The works of the early Church, the witnesses of the company of the Apostles, amongst whom are Saint Ignatius the God-bearer, a disciple of the Apostles and Saint Polycarp of Smyrna. These Fathers admonished the faithful of their day to safeguard themselves from the teachings of heretics and to maintain in the full only the Apostolic Tradition.

Eusebius of Caesarea, Ecclesiastical History, Bk 4:8

- Hegessipus, Eusebius tells us, attempted to collect the whole of the apostolic traditions and nearly managed it, gathering more than five books worth of material that Eusebius studied. Unfortunately, with the passage of time, these books were eventually lost.

2 The Elder here is referring to the well-known seven Oecumenical Councils, however, in essence the Church also accepts an eighth (879), which confirmed the rejection of the "filioque" clause in the presence and with the support of the Church of Rome, and a ninth (1341), which rejected the humanistic-scholastic theology of Barlaam in support of the Hesychasts and St. Gregory Palamas. The truths expounded by these two councils have helped to uphold the Church against the theological distortions which have been brought to bear over the past 650 years, first in the West, and soon thereafter in the East.

+202 AD
+215 AD

Stromatis, pg 7

- Saint Irenaeus and Clement of Alexandria inform us: "Those who explain Scripture without the help of the Church's Tradition cut asunder the significance of truth." Behold, further, those brilliant witnesses representing the faith of apostolic times and the period immediately following it up until the fourth century. The works of the ancient Church are an important testimony to the value of the Holy Tradition and honour shown it from those times until today.

+250 AD

- Origen says: "Preserve the Holy Tradition in the Church."

+403 AD

- St. Epiphanios writes: "It is necessary to hold to the Tradition because it is not possible for everything to be found in Holy Scripture. The Holy Apostles handed down some things via the written word, while they handed down others via the spoken word."

+407 AD

4th Homily on
2 Thess.;
see verse 2:45

- Saint John Chrysostom says: "Hence it is clear that the Holy Apostles did not deliver everything by epistle; rather many things they handed down via the spoken word, which is also trustworthy. If there is the Tradition, then do not ask for anything more."

+394 AD
Against
Eunomius,
Book 40

- Saint Gregory of Nyssa writes: "We have the Tradition set out for us from the Fathers like an inheritance by apostolic succession and transmitted via the saints."

+379 AD

On the
Holy Spirit

- Saint Basil the Great in his writings provides similar testimony. Here is how he expresses it: "Among the dogmas and *kerygma* (evangelical truths) that are safeguarded in the Church, some we have from the written teachings while others we have received orally from the Tradition of the Apostles by a concealed succession. The latter hold the same legitimacy and force as the written texts."

We must uphold with great reverence and godliness Holy Tradition, since not all that is needful to effect our salvation is found within Holy Scripture. Holy Scripture instructs us to do many things; however, it does not make manifest to us the light. For example, it instructs us to be baptized, but it does not explain to us the method. Likewise, it guides us to confess our sins, receive communion, and be crowned (married)—but nowhere does it specify the rite of carrying-out these *mysterion* (sacraments). Furthermore, it instructs us to pray, but does not tell us how, where and when. It tells us to make the sign of the Holy Cross in front of our chest according to the psalmist, "The light of Thy countenance, O Lord, hath been signed upon us; Thou hast given gladness to my heart," but it does not show us how. Who teaches us in writing to worship facing east? Where in Scripture are we told the words of the *epiclesis* (invocation) of the Holy Spirit for the sanctification of the all-holy Mysteries? Which teaching from Holy Scripture instructs us to bless the water of Baptism and the holy Unction of Holy Chrismation? Which passage in Scripture teaches us about the threefold denunciation and the renunciations of Satan before Holy Baptism? The prayer of glorification toward the Holy Trinity—"Glory to the Father and to the Son and to the Holy Spirit"—from which passage did it come to us?

Psalm 4:7

Posing these questions to the slanderer of Tradition, Saint Basil the Great says: "If we consent to abandon the unwritten traditions on the pretext that they do not have great worth, we err in great and elevated matters, rejecting the Gospel."

The ordering, therefore, by which the Church upholds the unwritten is: whatever is of apostolic descent and is practiced by the Fathers receives the validity of tradition and has the power of law in the Church of Christ. Accordingly, therefore, it must be safeguarded since its importance and benefit

The Rudder, Neamts Monastery, 1844, Canons 87, 91

springs from the relationship that exists between it and Holy Scripture. It is true that both have remained within a reciprocal unity and intimate relationship—a relationship based on the fact that both comprise the holy revelation of God and for us are the fount and source of Revelation. Hence, it is not possible for there to exist an inner contradiction between the two or for us to exclude one from the other. Holy Scripture possesses its unique witness of the scriptural canon and its dogmatic character (its divine inspiration) only in and with Holy Tradition, while Holy Tradition is able to prove the authenticity of its truth only together with Holy Scripture.

Icon from the School of Constantinople, 14th century (Byzantine Museum).

Archangel Michael
The Chief Commander of the Heavenly Hosts

CHAPTER 4

On the Veneration of the Saints and Angels

INQUIRER.: For what reason do we Orthodox venerate the angels and the saints and place them as intermediaries before God for our salvation? Certain people say that there is but one intercessor between God and man, Jesus Christ. The Apostle teaches the following concerning this subject: "For there is one God and one mediator between God and man, the man Jesus Christ." Consequently, neither the angels, nor the saints, nor anyone else except Christ is able to make intercession with God on behalf of our salvation.

1Tim. 2:5

ELDER CLEOPA: It is true that no one except Christ is able to intercede before the Father since only He presents Himself as a sacrifice for the salvation of the world. Accordingly, no one except for Christ is able to save man from sin. However, in honouring the saints, we do not put them in the place of Christ or even adjacent to Him. When the saints pray for us, it is precisely our salvation that they seek from Christ. They intercede with Him *for our salvation*; from Christ, they entreat our salvation. This is what we mean when we say that they intercede for us. By their *prayers,* the saints make petition for our salvation—not, however, as if they themselves have the power to save, for the only one who saves is Christ. Thus, we do *not* venerate the saints and angels as we do God. (That which we render the saints and angels is solely a veneration [προσκύνησις] of honour and reverence, while God we adore and worship [λατρεία] with perfect adoration, which is thus also properly called worship.[1]) We esteem the saints of God because they are friends and beloved of God, as it is written: "Ye are my friends, if ye do whatsoever I command you."

Jn. 15:14 While for Abraham likewise we read: "Abraham believed God, and it was imputed unto him for righteousness: and James 2:23 he was called the friend of God." The Apostle Paul writes to the Ephesians: "Now therefore ye are no more strangers and foreigners, but fellow citizens with the saints, and of the Eph. 2:19 household of God." Hence, as friends and beloved of God, we honour the saints. We also know that the saints have the Lk. 20:36 acclaim of God in the heavens. Indeed, they will judge the a 1 Cor. 4:2
a Mat. 19:23
a Heb. 12:22-
23 world.[a] While the saints were still found upon the earth, they had prophetic gifts[b] (for example, the prophecy of Elisha to b 1Kg 14:1-17
c 2Kg 5: 25-27 Gehazi[c]). Likewise, while being yet in this life, they prayed to God for the benefit of men, such as Abraham who prayed to God for his people.

The Orthodox New Testament, vol. 1, p. 81; Holy Apostles Convent, Buena Vista, CO., 1999

1 It is necessary to "make a distinction between absolute worship and adoration (λατρεία) and relative worship or veneration (προσκύνησις), which can be translated, lit., fall down or make obeisance or prostrate oneself or do reverence or venerate or pay homage. The Old Testament records many instances where the Patriarchs worship, venerate, make obeisance, and bow before people or places or things, but the latter is never with the worship or adoration due to God alone. The *proskynesis* given by a Christian to an icon is ontologically the same reverence he ought to give to his fellow Christians, who are images of Christ: but it is ontologically different from the *latreia* which is due to God alone. . . Note that the KJV translates the Greek word *proskynesis* with 'worship' and the word *latreia* with 'serve.'" [Cf. St. John of Damascus, On the Divine Images, 9-11.]

INQ.: How is it that the saints and angels are able to mediate with God on behalf of the salvation of men, since we must await our salvation from Christ who is the Saviour and mediator of our salvation? Thus it is written: "Neither is there salvation in any other: for there is none other name under heaven given among men, whereby we must be saved." There is no need, then, to resort to the saints if we wish to inherit salvation.

Acts 4:12

EC: On the contrary, this work of the saints is of great importance. They have the ability to pray before God on behalf of man and his salvation. This is most clearly evident from the passage from the Book of Revelation, which states: "And when he had taken the book, the four beasts and the four and twenty elders fell down before the Lamb, having every one of them harps, and golden vials full of odours, which are the prayers of saints."

Rev. 5:8

The saints pray for men not only in the heavens after their repose, but also while they are in this world, as we pointed out previously. Namely, Abraham prayed for Abimelech, Moses for his people, and also the Apostle Paul for his disciples. Thus he wrote: "We give thanks to God always for you all, making mention of you in our prayers; Remembering without ceasing your works of faith . . . in the sight of God and our Father." And elsewhere: "Wherefore we also pray always for you, that our God would count you worthy of this calling . . ." And again: "[I] cease not to give thanks for you, making mention of you in my prayers, that God . . . may give unto you the spirit of wisdom . . ." Still elsewhere: "And this we also pray for, even your perfection." And to Timothy he writes: "I thank God, whom I serve from my forefathers with pure conscience, that without ceasing I have remembrance of thee in my prayers night and day."

1 Thess. 1:2-3

2 Thess. 1:11

Eph. 1:16-17
2 Cor. 13:9

2 Tim. 1:3

In addition to this, in the Old Testament it is written: "And my servant Job shall pray for you; for him will I accept, lest I deal with you after your folly in that ye have not spoken unto me the thing which is right, like My servant Job." And likewise, the Prophet Daniel, enraptured in vision and praying to God, says: "He is my beloved brother, the prophet of God, Jeremiah, which prays often for the people and the holy city." Observe that from all this, it clearly appears that the saints have the power to intercede with God for our salvation, revealing the fact that, as much in this life as also after their death, they pray to heaven for our souls' benefit. Likewise, God sends his angels to help those that pray to Him. God sent His angel to Daniel to deliver him from the mouths of lions. And the great Apostle Paul says that the angels are attendants of God, those whom He will send in order to help them that will inherit His salvation. Whosoever receives the angels receives Christ. Thus, from all of the above written testimonies, it is known that the angels and saints are able to intercede with God for us by their prayers since they are friends, beloved and dear to God.

Inq.: I have heard some say that the Orthodox, by the veneration and reverence that they bestow upon the saints and the angels, eclipse the glory and honour that belongs to God alone. The Apostle Paul sternly rebukes and chastises the Colossians that did this, leaving the worship of God and venerating the angels. Here is what he wrote: "Let no man beguile you of your reward in a voluntary humility and worshipping of angels . . . and not holding the Head (Christ) from which all the body by joints and bands having nourishment ministered, and knit together, increaseth with the increase of God."

Job 42:8

Dan. 10:11-21

Gen. 24:7

Dan. 6:22

Heb. 1:14

Mat. 10:40-41

Col. 2:18-19

EC: No eclipse or depreciation of the glory of God results from the reverence and veneration of His angels. This is so, first of all, because the veneration (worshipful) that we offer to God is one thing and the veneration (honourable) that we render to the angels and saints of God is another. The same Holy Spirit exhorts us to glorify God with His saints, saying "Praise ye God in His saints."[2] Thus, we glorify God likewise when we seek in prayer the help and mediation of the angels and saints since the saints, in their succession, convey our supplications and requests together with their own prayers to God.

Ps. 150:1

Acts 9:32-42, 20:36, 28:3-9

Rev. 5:8

Rom. 2:10

God Himself glorified His saints and robed them with His glory: "And the glory which thou gavest me I have given them; that they may be one, even as we are one." Elsewhere He says: "He that receiveth you receiveth me; and he that receiveth me receiveth him that sent me. He that receiveth a prophet in the name of a prophet shall receive a prophet's reward; and he that receiveth a righteous man in the name of a righteous man shall receive a righteous man's reward." These testimonies prove sufficiently enough the delusion of those who repudiate the honour shown toward the saints and angels (those beloved servants of God)—not realizing that in practice they turn their back on God Himself, the Creator and Fashioner of saints.

Jn. 17:22

Mat. 10:40-41

INQ.: Why do not the saints, then, if they are really able, entreat God for our salvation? For example, Abraham had no wish to entreat God on behalf of the merciless rich man. Was it perhaps because he did not ask insistently?

2 The Greek reads ἐν τοῖς ἁγίοις (ἅγιος) "set apart to or by God, consecrated; holy, morally pure, upright." The KJV renders ἁγίοις here as "sanctuary."

EC: Abraham did not intercede for the rich man because during the time of his life he never sought the help of the saints, nor even lifted his mind toward God. In the Acts of the Apostles, we see that the Apostle Peter objected to the worship that Cornelius rendered him inasmuch as he is but a man. The Roman centurion had become acquainted with the notion of God since turning away from the idols. Consequently, it was quite natural for him to believe Peter, as a man sent by God, to be like God or surely as a man superior to others or like a demigod that deserved not reverence but worship like unto the gods. For this reason, Peter rejected the worship that Cornelius sought to offer him.

In a passage of the Acts of the Apostles, the Apostles Paul and Barnabas rebuked those who offered them worship for the same reason as given above, inasmuch as they considered them gods and were preparing to worship them. From these passages, we see that the inhabitants of the city of Lystra, amazed by Paul's miraculous healing of the man lame from his birth, with one voice cried out: "The gods are come down to us in the likeness of men. And they called Barnabas 'Zeus,' and Paul 'Hermes,' since he was the chief speaker." Thus, it is easy to understand the refusal of the Apostles to be worshipped as gods, since they preached against the false gods and led all to the worship of the One and only God. "And with these words, they scarcely restrained the people from offering sacrifice to them."

In another passage, the angel who explains the apocalyptic dream refuses the worship that the Apostle and Evangelist John offers him, reasoning thus: "I am thy fellow servant . . ." That is, "I am like unto you, a servant of God, as you are. We are in a relationship of equality and I ought not receive

Acts 10:25-26

Acts 14:3-15

Acts 14:8-12

Acts 14:18

Rev. 19:10

Rev. 1:10

worship from you, most of all since you are here also, not in body but in spirit: i.e. in an angelic state; in that, you are like me with the "spirit of prophecy" which looks to bear witness to Christ."

Additional grounds for refutation are found represented by the words of the angel: "Worship God." God was in their midst and the angel, who was unveiled, would have slighted Him if he had received worship from John for himself. It is exactly the same between men: it is an insult to pay more honour to a highly respected politician in the presence of the president of the country. Indeed, when he is present, the courtesy and honour in all things is assigned to him who is superior to others. Yet, this does not mean that those highly regarded close to him are not also worthy of honour.

Rev. 22:8-9

Furthermore, in a subsequent passage, the angel expresses—this time more clearly—his equality with the Apostle John and the negligence and impiety he would have shown if he had received worship.

Thus, the invocation of the above passages by some to justify their false teachings, namely, the renunciation of granting veneration to the saints and angels, is shown to be an interpretation all their own and of their own making. The Apostles Peter, Paul, and Barnabas forbade the people to worship them as gods because, as holy men, it was only appropriate for them to receive a veneration of honour and reverence from other men. Likewise, the unveiled angel refused the veneration of John by virtue of the equality that he shared with him since John also was a servant of God. It is not hard to demonstrate within many passages of Scripture the honour and reverence shown by men to the saints and angels of God as well as the latter's acceptance of such veneration.

Similar to the first example, we relate the following: King Ahaziah sent a captain of the third fifty with his fifty men to kneel before Elijah and to beseech him. When they came to him, the captain spoke to him and said to him: "O man of God, I pray thee, let my life and the life of these other

2 Kg. 1:13

fifty, thy servants, be precious in thy sight." And a little later: " . . . the sons of the prophets who were in view at Jericho . . . came to meet him, and prostrated (προσεκύνησαν) themselves to the ground before him." Again, in another place: "Then

2 Kg. 2:15

King Nebuchadnezzar fell upon his face and worshipped

Dan. 2:46

(προσεκύνησε) Daniel." We also witness that Balaam, bowing down his face, venerated (προσεκύνησε) the Angel of the Lord: "Then the Lord opened the eyes of Balaam, and he saw the Angel of the Lord standing in the way and his sword drawn in his hand: and he bowed down his head, and fell flat on his

Num. 22:31
Gen. 19:1

face." The Angel of the Lord accepted the veneration of Lot. The Angel of the Lord received the veneration of Manoah and his wife, who fell on their faces to the ground, while the

Jdg. 13:18-21

Angel of the Lord ascended in the flame of the altar. The Angel of the Lord received veneration from David and the

1 Chr. 16-18
Dan. 10:9-15

priests of the people. And so too did the Angel of the Lord accept veneration from the Prophet Daniel.

Behold, in all that I have answered you, in all that you had trouble believing, the saints and angels of God do not receive worship (λατρεία) from men. Read with care the relevant passages of Holy Scripture and you will understand clearly that both the saints of God and His angels do receive honour from men without this honour rousing any anger in God. For how is it possible for God to be angry upon seeing His precious and beloved friends being magnified in His Name when

He Himself has glorified them, endowed them with
Rom. 2:10 wonderworking power, and granted them exceptional
spiritual gifts?

INQ.: What are these spiritual gifts and exceptional
powers with which God has honoured His Saints?

Psalm 67:36 **EC:** From the beginning, He gave them the power to
work miracles, as it is written: "Wondrous is God in
Psalm 15:3 His saints, even the God of Israel" and "In the saints
that are in His earth hath the Lord been wondrous; He
a Ex. 10:12 hath wrought all His desires in them."
b Ex. 7:20-21
c Ex. 8:6   Surely, with the hand of the Prophet Moses, did God
d Ex. 8:12 not smite Egypt,[a] transform water into blood,[b] bring
e Ex. 9:3 frogs,[c] gnats,[d] pestilence to the animals,[e] scathing
f Ex. 9:9,18,23 blisters, hail and fire,[f] locusts,[g] darkness,[h] death to the
g Ex. 10:4-6
h Ex. 10:21 firstborn infants,[i] pass the Israelites through the Red
i Ex. 12:29-30 Sea,[j] destroy Pharaoh and his army,[k] and carry the defeat
j Ex. 14:16 of Amalek,[l] make sweet the waters of Marah,[m] and gush
k Ex. 14:27
l Ex. 17 forth water from the rock in Horeb,[n] cause the earth
m Ex. 15 to swallow up Korah and Dathan,[o] send a cure via the
n Ex. 17:6 brass serpent,[p] and cause water to spout forth from the
o Num 16:28,31
p Num. 21 rock at Kadesh?[q]
q Num. 20   Next, with Joshua the son of Nun, He wrought these
r Josh. 3:11-17
s Josh. 6:6-20 miraculous events: the restraint of the waters of the Jordan,[r]
t Jdg.14,16:28-31 the collapse of the walls of Jericho.[s] And with Gideon: the
u 1 Sam.12:16-18
v 1 Kg. 17:1 destruction of the inhabitants of Midian. With Samson:
w 1 Kg. 17:4 the tearing to pieces of the lion and the pulling down of
the house of the god Dagon.[t] And with Samuel: the light-
ning flashes and the peals of thunder with the reaping at
harvest-time.[u] With the Prophet Elijah: the great drought,[v]
the flour and oil of the widow,[w] the resurrection of the son

of the widow at Zarephath,[a] fire from heaven upon the sacrifice,[b] the opening up of heaven and the great rain.[c] Further, we see the chastisement of Ahaziah with death,[d] as well as the separation of the waters of the Jordan with the mantle of Elijah. Then, with Elisha we have: the parting of the waters of Jordan,[e] the purification of the waters of Jericho,[f] the killing of the children of Bethel by two she-bears,[g] the resurrection of the Shunammite's son,[h] the healing of Naaman,[i] the chastisement of Gehazi with leprosy,[j] and the resurrection of a man through the bones of Elisha.[k] And with Isaiah: the healing of Hezekiah.[l]

The Holy Twelve Apostles bear witness that they rendered all sorts of healings.[m] So too the Seventy Apostles accomplished divers miracles.[n] Still further, innumerable miracles are made reference to as brought about by the Apostles[o]—such as the healing of the man lame from his birth,[p] the death of Ananias and Sapphira,[q] the healing of the sick,[r] the healing of the bedridden Aeneas,[s] the resurrection of Tabitha,[t] the recovery of the sight of Saul Paul,[u] the chastisement of Elymas the sorcerer,[v] the resurrection of the youth Eutychus,[w] the healing of the father of Publius,[x] and many other countless miracles, signs and wonders of which there is no space here to recount them all.

a 1 Kg. 17:17-23
b 1 Kg. 18:36-38
c 1 Kg. 18:41-46
d 2 Kg. 1:16
e 2 Kg. 2:14
f 2 Kg. 2:19-22
g 2 Kg. 2:23
h 2 Kg. 4:32-35
i 2 Kg. 5:10-14
j 2Kg. 5:20-27
k 2 Kg. 13:21
l 2 Kg. 20:1-7
m Mat. 10:1,
m Mk. 3:14-15
m Mk. 6:7-13
m Lk. 9:1-6
n Lk. 10:9,17
o Mk. 16:20,
o Acts 2:43
o Acts 5:12-16
p Acts 3:2-8
q Acts 5:1-10
r Acts 5:16
s Acts 9:34
t Acts 9:36-41
u Acts 9:17-18
v Acts 13:11
w Acts 20:9-12
x Acts 28:8

Look, my brother, with what power and grace-filled gifts God endowed His saints, both in the Old and the New Testament! Therefore, now in the back of your mind, concerning the miracles of the saints of God, review that which was spoken by the Holy Spirit: "Wondrous is God in His saints, even the God of Israel."

Ps. 67:35

If we also honour the angels of God in like manner with His saints, we must confess that God has shown to the world many extraordinary miracles via His holy angels. We have

a Ex. 14:19,
23:20, 32:34,
33:2
a Num. 20:16
b Gen. 19:13
c 1 Chr. 21:14-16
d 2 Kg. 19:35
e Acts 12:23
f Mat. 1:30 1
g Lk. 1:31
h Mat. 28:5-7
i Acts 1:10
j Mat. 4:11
j Mk. 1:13
k Lk. 2:9
l Mat. 13:39-42,
24:31

many examples: the Angel of the Lord leading the Israelites out of Egypt,[a] the destruction of Sodom and Gomorrah, which was effected by angels,[b] the epidemic in Jerusalem,[c] the destruction of the army of the Assyrians,[d] the chastisement through death of Herod,[e] and the announcement of the angel of the births of Jesus Christ[f] and John the Baptist,[g] of the Resurrection of Christ,[h] and of the Ascension and Second Coming of Christ.[i] Moreover, the angels ministered unto Jesus Christ Himself,[j] they announced to the shepherds His birth,[k] and they will separate the just from the unjust on the Day of Judgement.[l] Indeed, countless signs and miraculous wonders have come to pass via the holy angels of God, are even now being accomplished, and will yet be shown forth until the end of the ages.

2 Pet. 2:11
Jude 1:9
Ps. 67:17, 90:11,
102:21 etc.

These works of God's love are brought about by Him through the service of His holy angels. Hence, we are duty-bound to honour the holy angels since, with love and obedience, they serve the work of our salvation.

Icon from the Holy Monastery of Vatopedi, Mount Athos (13th century).

Most-Holy Theotokos – the Directress

"Whatsoever He saith unto you, do it." (Jn. 2:5)

CHAPTER 5

On the Veneration of the Ever-Virgin Mary

INQUIRER: Concerning the Mother of Jesus Christ, Mary: Why do Orthodox Christians honour her so much and venerate her in the same way as they venerate God?

ELDER CLEOPA: We do honour the All-Holy Virgin Mary and Birth-giver of God (Theotokos[1]) more than the other holy saints and angels; yet, nevertheless, we do not ascribe to her the same veneration as we do to God.

The veneration that we render unto her is called honorific and reverential, as she is the Mother of the Lord, having not only a spiritual relationship with Him, as happens with other

---

1 The title "Theotokos" (God-bearer) is witnessed to by many from the earliest days of the Church: Righteous Elizabeth was the first to address Mary as "the Mother of my Lord" (Lk. 1:43). St. Athanasios the Great (296-373) used the title "Theotokos" thus: "He took flesh of a virgin, Mary Theotokos, bearer of God, and was made Man" (*Discourse Against the Arians*). St. Gregory the Theologian (4th century) says: "If anyone does not accept the holy Mary as Theotokos, he is without the Godhead" (Epistle 101). At the Third Oecumenical Council (431 AD) in Ephesus the title "Theotokos" was formally defended and held to be sacred. And St. John of Damascus says: "It is with justice and truth that we call Mary the 'Mother of God.' For this name, 'Theotokos,' embraces the whole mystery of the dispensation" (*Exposition of the Orthodox Faith*, bk. iii, ch. xii.)

saints, but also a physical union with Him. For this reason, we chant in the Church's hymn to her: "It is truly meet to call thee blessed, the Theotokos, the ever-blessed and all-immaculate, and Mother of our God. More honourable than the Cherubim, and beyond compare more glorious than the Seraphim, thee who without corruption gavest birth to God the Word, the very Theotokos, thee do we magnify." She is higher than the saints and the angels, and therefore from angels and saints she receives veneration. Thus, it was that

Lk. 1:28-29

the Archangel Gabriel venerated her in the Annunciation. And in the same manner did Elizabeth, the Mother of Saint

Lk. 1:40-43

John the Baptist, also venerate her. The Holy Virgin herself prophesied in the Holy Spirit that all generations would honour her: "for behold, from henceforth all generations shall call me blessed. For He that is mighty hath done to me great

Lk. 1:48-49

things. . . " Hence, the honour rendered her is according to the will of God.

INQ.: I have heard some say that we should not ascribe great honour to the Virgin Mary, since even her own Son, Jesus Christ, did not honour her. This is apparent from the words of the Saviour, which the holy Evangelist relates in the following passage: "Then one said to Him, 'Behold, Thy mother and Thy brethren stand outside, desiring to speak with Thee.' But He answered and said unto him that told him, 'Who is My mother? And who are My brethren?' And He stretched forth His hand toward His disciples and said, 'Behold, My mother and My brethren! For whosoever shall do the will of My Father who is in Heaven, the same is My brother, and sister, and mother.'" Consequently, the fact that the

Mat. 12:47-50

Virgin Mary was His mother holds no great significance. In the sight of Christ, natural blood ties and human relations do not have any importance or priority over spiritual fellowship with those who do the will of the Father, whosoever they may be.

EC: This is written for another special reason that, excepting the natural human kinship, there exists above all another relationship with Christ much higher and more important—the spiritual relationship—which consists in doing the will of God. This kind of relation, however, does not abolish and does not discard the natural one. The difference consists only in that the spiritual relationship can be acquired by anyone who puts into practice the will of God. A relationship refers not only to human blood-relations, but also to unity through spiritual love and relations of the soul. Whoever does the will of God spiritually becomes a relative of God. Thus, with the above words, the Saviour neither brushed aside His natural relations and kinship with His Mother, nor rejected the honour befitting a mother from her Son, but only sought to elevate the other—the spiritual relationship—with Him, which is of greater value and can, furthermore, be acquired by each believer. Accordingly, it was a word of exhortation and encouragement that was directed to the others and not a word of dishonour toward His Mother. As long as our Saviour Jesus Christ was with His Mother on the earth, He always listened to her and loved her, and He did not exhibit disobedience toward her in anything that she asked of Him. Hence, at the wedding in Cana of Galilee, at the request of His Mother, He performed His first miracle, changing water into wine. He took great care of His Mother, such that even while He hung crucified on the Cross, He entrusted her to the care of the most beloved of His disciples, the Evangelist John, as the text says: "When Jesus therefore saw His mother and the disciple standing by whom He loved, He said unto His mother, 'Woman, behold thy son!' Then He said to the disciple, 'behold thy mother!'" You see that even in the most difficult time of His suffering on the Cross, the Saviour does not neglect to care for His Mother who gave birth to Him

Lk. 2:51

Jn. 2:3-10

Jn. 19:26-27

and raised Him. And how, I wonder, could it be possible for Him to scorn or disdain His Mother when God Himself commands us to honour mother and father, as it is written: "Honour thy father and thy mother"?

Dt. 5:16

INQ.: All right, but why do we then call Mary "ever-virgin" when at the same time her Son Himself calls her "woman," which means that she was married and not a virgin, as it thus stands to reason from the word of Scripture: "When Jesus therefore saw His mother and the disciple standing by whom He loved, He said unto His mother, 'Woman, behold thy son!' He addresses her in the same bluntly disdainful manner at the wedding in Cana of Galilee: "Woman, what have I to do with thee?"[2] For this reason, neither can we consider her as someone greater, nor can we offer to her special veneration and honour.

Jn. 19:26

Jn. 2:4

EC: In the first passage, in no case is a disdainful word spoken.[3] On the contrary, it is clear how, from natural disposition, He makes sure to entrust her to the protection of the Apostle John, knowing that He would no longer remain on earth, that for the rest of her life she would be under his protection and care. This is not an action of scornfulness, but truly an act of great honour and great veneration toward His Mother, for even while suffering on His Cross He did not forget to care for her. And if He called her "woman," in no way did He say it to mean a married woman[4] or as a sign of disrespect, but only in the sense of gender and of sex. For

---

2 John 2:4, (τί ἐμοὶ καὶ σοὶ γύναι) should read "What is it to Me and to thee, woman?" in English, not "Woman, what have I to do with thee?" as the KJV has rendered it.

3 In fact, the word "γύναι" which Christ uses here is noted by Liddle & Scott (Abridged Edition, p. 147) as being, "a term of respect, mistress, lady . . .".

4 Mary was not married, but was betrothed to Joseph. The inquirer is implying with the phrase "married woman" that she was not a virgin when in fact, as St. Irenaeos expresses it, "Mary, having a man betrothed to her, but nonetheless a virgin, was obedient and became to herself and to the whole human race a cause of salvation."

Against Heresies, bk. iii, ch. xxii

that is exactly how the two angels spoke to Mary Magdalene at the tomb: "Woman, why weepest thou?" And the two men who appeared at the Ascension of the Lord into heaven said to the Apostles: "Ye men of Galilee, why stand ye gazing up into heaven?" Neither the angels nor the two men said the words "woman" and "men" with scornfulness but rather, on the contrary, in a kind manner.

Jn. 20:12-13

Acts 1:11

INQ.: Granted, but where is it said in Holy Scripture that Mary, the Mother of Jesus, was a virgin, and even ever-virgin, as the Orthodox faithful refer to her?

EC: That in truth she gave birth as a virgin, Holy Scripture discloses to us in the following way. When the Archangel Gabriel came to Nazareth and announced to her that she would bear the Son of God, entering into her house, he called to her: "Hail, thou that art highly favoured, the Lord is with thee; blessed art thou among women." And looking at him she was frightened by his words and thought within herself: "What manner of salutation is this?" And the angel said to her: "Fear not, Mary, for thou hast found favour with God. And behold, thou shalt conceive in thy womb and bring forth a Son, and shalt call His name JESUS. He shall be great and shall be called the Son of the Highest; and the Lord God shall give unto Him the throne of His father David, and He shall reign over the house of Jacob for ever; and of His kingdom there shall be no end." Then Mary said unto the angel, "How shall this be, seeing I know not a man?" And the angel answered and said unto her, "The Holy Spirit shall come upon thee, and the power of the Highest shall overshadow thee. Therefore also that Holy Being who shall be born of thee shall be called the Son of God."

Lk. 1:35

Lk. 1:28

You heard that the archangel venerated the Virgin Mary, calling her "full of grace" and "blessed among women," that

Lk. 1:29-35

she had great grace from God, that she had never known a man, that she was overshadowed by the power of the Most High, and that she conceived and gave birth to the Son of God by the Holy Spirit. You also heard that although she was a virgin, as she had never known a man, the angel did not say to her "blessed art thou among virgins" but "blessed art thou among women," without this word expressing disdain for the Most Holy Theotokos—she who is "full of grace" and revealed mystically from olden times: "And I will put enmity between thee and the woman, and between thy seed and her Seed; It shall bruise thy head, and thou shalt bruise His heel." It is she who was given to be the mystical and spiritual Eve and to give birth to Christ, the New Adam, He who would bring true life into the world. The divine fathers of the Church tell us that Christ is called "Seed of the woman" because He was not born by sperm of man but by the Holy Spirit and from the most holy blood of the All-Holy Virgin He took His flesh.

Gen. 3:15

Gen. 3:15

On the great day of the future Judgement, this Queen and Virgin, Mary, will sit on the right of her Son with great and inexpressible glory, as the psalm reveals: "At Thy right hand stood the queen, arrayed in a vesture of inwoven gold, adorned in varied colours." Seeing that the Archangel Gabriel called her woman (knowing her to be a virgin), saying "blessed art thou among women," how is it that you still suppose the Virgin Mary was married?

Psalm 44:10

Nonetheless, consider this also: when God created Eve from the side of Adam, and led her to him and he named her woman, was Eve thus married just because Adam called her woman? Likewise, wasn't Eve a virgin since she was created from the virgin body of Adam without him having physical relations with a woman? Thus, if Eve was created virgin by God, and if God Himself, along with Adam, called this virgin

Gen. 2:21-22

Gen. 2:23

"woman," how is it that later He calls Mary "woman" with the meaning—as you maintain—of a married woman? The meaning differs within this one word to such a degree?

God, as much as Adam, called Eve "woman" when she was a virgin because she had a female, and not male, nature, showing thus the feminine sex. In no way is it understood that God and Adam called her who was received from the side of Adam (and was still a virgin) a woman with the meaning of married woman. For just as Eve was a virgin when he called her woman, so too the mystical and spiritual Eve, the most holy Virgin Mary—she who gave birth to Christ the New Adam—is virgin unto the ages of ages, even though Holy Scripture refers to her as woman. At that time, Adam, by the will of God and in virginity, gave birth from his body to a woman, yet not by sexual intercourse with a woman. When the fullness of time had come, the female nature in synergy with the Holy Spirit gave birth to a man, yet not by relations with a man. In virginity, the Virgin Mary gave birth and remained virgin—just as in the beginning, in virginity, Adam gave birth without the co-operation of a woman, remaining virgin. Thus, God deigned through the Virgin Mary to cure the fallen nature of the old Adam with the New Adam born of the Virgin[5]. He came into the world and was invested with our nature out of inexpressible goodness and mercy, in order to redeem the old Adam along with his whole race from punishment and death. "For God so loved the world that He gave His only begotten Son, that whosoever believeth in Him should not perish, but have everlasting life." Thus, pay close attention: Holy Scripture does not call the

Jn. 3:16

St. Justin Martyr, *Dialogue with Trypo*, ch. 100

5 "Eve, being a virgin and incorrupt, conceived the word spoken of the serpent, and brought forth disobedience and death. But Mary the Virgin answered, 'May it be according to Thy word,' and received faith and grace."

Lk. 1:43

Mother of God woman and thereby mean married woman, as some believe, but with the word woman reveals only the sex, the given female nature of the Ever-Virgin Mary, while simultaneously (in a hidden or concealed manner) saying that she is the woman whose Seed (Christ) will bruise the head of the serpent and through whom shall come the salvation of mankind.

In addition to the above, we should add the following:

- In that the Virgin Mary was the Mother of the Saviour, she was granted the greatest honour a human being could receive.

- When, by the Holy Spirit, she conceived in her womb the Saviour of the world, she was completely pure of every sin, more so than any human being, no matter how holy he might be.

- Moreover, the honour to be shown the Ever-virgin Mary has been prophesied by God, a similar honour having never been shown to any other human being, and thus it is proper that she be considered the first among the saints, just as John the Baptist was the greatest among the Prophets.

Mal. 3:1

Is. 40:3

On account of all that has been said, the Holy Virgin Mary should be venerated with the greatest honour and piety among the saints, inasmuch as she is the Queen and the crown of all the saints. As it concerns the truth of her remaining a virgin after the birth of the Saviour, see the prophecies of Ezekiel, which refer to her.

Ezk. 44:1-3

INQ.: From what has been presented, we can see and believe that, indeed, the Virgin and Mother of Jesus Christ, Mary, remained forever a virgin and that—besides Jesus—she never had other children. All the same, it is written in Scripture that Joseph "knew her not until she had brought forth her first-born Son." This seems to imply that afterward she could have had other children.

EC: Indeed, Holy Scripture does say: "and knew her not until she had brought forth her first-born Son. And he called His name JESUS." Yet, be attentive, for in Holy Scripture, the phrase ἕως οὗ ("until when") means eternally.[6] The Lord says, "And lo, I am with you always, even *unto* (ἕως) the end of the world." Does this mean that the Lord will depart from us at the end of the world? Listen to what the divine Apostle Paul says: "And so shall we ever be with the Lord." And in another place of Holy Scripture it is written: "The Lord said unto my Lord: Sit Thou at My right hand, *until* I make Thine enemies the footstool of Thy feet." Could it be that this means our Saviour Jesus Christ will not sit at the right hand of the Father and reign with Him unto the ages of ages? We know very well that "of His Kingdom there shall be no end." In another place of Holy Scripture, when speaking about Noah, it says, "he sent forth a raven, which went forth

Mat. 1:25

Mat. 28:20

1 Thess. 4:17

Psalm 109:1

Lk. 1:33

See: The Orthodox New Testament, vol. 1, p. 76; Holy Apostles Convent, Buena Vista, CO., 1999

Homily iv, Commentary on St. Matthew

Homily ii on the Dormition

6 "He was not knowing her until" (καὶ οὐκ ἐγίνωσκεν αὐτὴν ἕως) Note the imperfect tense, continuous or linear action, "he was not knowing" or "he kept on not knowing." Saint John Chrysostom: "He uses the word 'until,' not that thou shouldest suspect that afterwards he did come to know her, but in order that thou mayest learn that before the birth the Virgin was wholly untouched. But on what account did he say 'until'? Because it is usual in Scripture oftentimes to do this, and to use this expression without reference to limited times. . . .
When discoursing also of God, Scripture says, "From the age until the age Thou art [Ps. 89(90):2]," not as fixing limits in this case. . . . So then here likewise, it uses the word 'until,' to make certain what was before the birth, but as to what follows, it leaves thee to make the inference." Saint John of Damascus: "While every virgin loses her virginity in bringing forth, she was a virgin before her delivery, a virgin in her delivery, and a virgin after she brought forth."

Gen. 8:7
to and fro, *until* the waters were dried up from the earth." Does this mean that the raven returned at one point to the ark? But we know that the raven never returned. Again, elsewhere, it is seen that Michal, daughter of Saul and wife of David "had no child *unto* the day of her death." Does this mean that she gave birth to children after her death, since it 2 Sam. 6:23 says, "*unto* the day of her death"?

Therefore, open and fix your intellectual eyes upon these three important testimonies, which are representative of many others found in Holy Scripture, and understand that the phrase ἕως οὗ in Scripture conveys the meaning of eternity. Thus, the Saviour will be eternally with His Apostles and with all those who have kept His commandments, and He will stand on the right hand of the Father sharing in His eternal reign. Thus, the raven will never return to the Ark of Noah; and Michal, the daughter of Saul, after her death, will never acquire children. And in this way exactly, the just and God-fearing Joseph never knew she who was a virgin—a virgin before the birth of Christ, during the bearing of Christ, and after the birth of Christ—the most holy and most pure Virgin Mary, Theotokos and Mother of the Light, the Queen of angels and of the race of man.

Furthermore, we can add the observation that the expression ἕως οὗ does not refer strictly to the duration of the condition of Mary's virginity, but, on the contrary, is used to emphasize precisely the fact that Jesus Christ was born of the Virgin without a man. For this reason, some editions of the New Testament prefer the translation, "without Joseph knowing her, Mary gave birth to her only Son," which means the same thing, as we showed above.[7]

INQ.: Many places are found in Holy Scripture that testify to

---

7 The Elder is evidently speaking of translations from Greek into Romanian.

Icon from the Catholicon of the Holy Monastery of Stavronikita, Mount Athos, Greece.

The Annunciation of the
Most-Holy Theotokos

"Behold the handmaid of the Lord;
be it unto me according to thy word."

the fact that Christians do not have more than one mediator for their salvation, Jesus Christ. And yet, we appeal to the Mother of the Lord, saying: "We have no other hope besides thee" and "Most holy Theotokos, save us." According to some, this is a great error since we place the Theotokos, like the Saviour, as a mediator for our salvation.

EC: As concerns this question, I provided you with a clear explanation when we were speaking about the veneration of the saints. When we turn to the Mother of the Lord with the expression, "we have no other hope besides thee," what are we deprived of? With this, we do not deny the uniqueness of Christ as mediator of our *objective* salvation, yet neither are we indifferent to the rendering of any sort of help related to our *personal* salvation. The meaning of this expression is see chapter 13 as follows: "You can give us the most help for our personal salvation" or "another superior helper we cannot find, nor one among the saints." Or, "We have none other who is able to help us as much as you, O Mother of the Saviour."

As for the expression of prayer that is addressed to her, "Most holy Theotokos, save us," it means: "Entreat your Son to save us," or "Redeem us." In the Greek language, in which almost all of the books of the New Testament are written as well as the liturgical books of the Orthodox Church, the word "save" means to redeem from evil, temptations, distress, and necessity. Consequently, it means: "Help us by your prayer to be redeemed from evil, from the works of the devil, from our passions." Therefore, by "save us", we do not mean "forgive us our sins," but "entreat your Son for our salvation." It is impossible for the veneration of the Mother of the Lord to exceed the reverence shown to her Son, for Whom we have not decreased in the least the worship due Him. On the contrary, all veneration shown to the Mother of God is a constituent part of the veneration shown her Son, Who chose her and blessed her to be His Mother. This I have shown you with the testimony of the Scriptures, about the honour, glory, and grace that God gave to His Most Holy Mother.

Nevertheless, consider also that God, after the fall of Adam and Eve, foretold that the Mother of the Lord would be a "woman-virgin," who with Her Son would slay the head of the dragon. Afterward, concerning her, He prophesied that this virgin would give birth to Emmanuel-God. It is she who would mediate the advent in the world of our Saviour Jesus Christ. It is to her that the Archangel Gabriel showed veneration, calling her "full of grace" and "blessed art thou among women." She is the one that Elizabeth, the mother of Saint John the Baptist, venerated—calling out: "blessed art thou among women" and "Mother of my Lord." Blessed are the womb and the breasts that sustained and nursed Christ, the Saviour of the world. The Saviour, her Son, showed her obedience, the first miracle happened in Cana of Galilee at her request, and Christ cared for her even when undergoing His fearful sufferings on the Cross, entrusting her to the care of the most beloved of His Apostles. She herself prophesied in the Holy Spirit that all generations would call her blessed and would offer her honourable veneration for the glory which, on account of her humility, God has granted her. Her name itself means "Madame, Lady" in the Jewish language. This Lady and Queen Virgin will be standing on the right hand of the throne of Her Son at the Last Judgement. By the Holy Spirit, she was pregnant with and gave birth to the Son of God—as she had been overshadowed by the strength of His power from above—and remained a virgin after giving birth. She is more honourable than the Cherubim and beyond compare more glorious than the Seraphim ("It is truly meet…"), not having other children besides Jesus Christ, the

Gen. 3:15

Is. 7:13

Jer. 32:2-23

Lk. 1:28

Lk. 1:40-43

Lk. 11:27-28

Lk. 2:51

Jn. 2:3-10

Jn. 19:26-27

Lk. 1:48-49

Lk. 1:35

Ezk. 44:1-3

Jn. 12:13

Saviour of the world. The mother of those who are called the "brothers and sisters of the Lord" is not the Mother of the Lord, as also the brothers of the Lord are only His relatives and not His natural brothers.

Therefore, how can we not honour the Mother of God when Scripture itself shows us that even the Archangel Gabriel esteemed her as worthy of honourable veneration?

Lk. 1:29

How can we not venerate the Theotokos who is the Church of the King of Glory and is glorified above the heavens, since she bore in her womb God, whose glory can be contained neither in heaven nor on earth? For this reason, we venerate the Mother of God who, according to the testimonies of Scripture and of the Evangelist, is "full of grace." Likewise, for this reason, the Theotokos is considered a woman of great virtue, for she had grace from God and was blessed among women.

If we truly believe that which is written in Holy Scripture, we must honour and respect the Mother of the Lord, for Scripture tells us that all generations of nations will bless her

Lk. 1:48-49

for the glory with which God adorned her.

The Most-Holy Virgin

Icon from the Catholicon of the Holy Monastery of Stavronikita, Mt. Athos, Greece.

The Prophet Isaiah prophesying of the Nativity
of Christ from the Most Holy Theotokos.

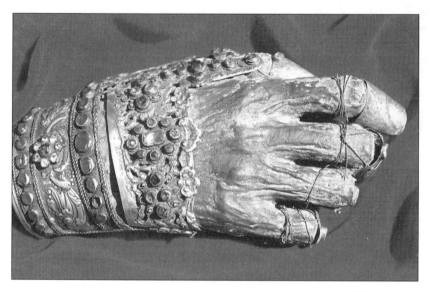

The incorrupt right hand of Saint John Chrysostom (407 AD),
treasured at the Holy Monastery of Philotheou, Mount Athos, Greece.

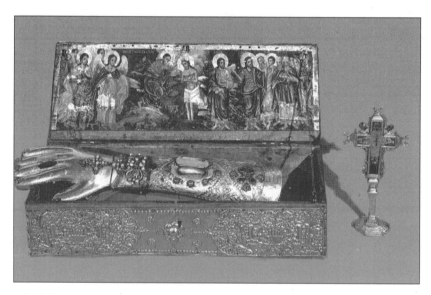

The holy and incorrupt right hand of Saint John the Baptist (which baptized the
Lord Jesus Christ) within its protective casing, treasured at the Holy Monastery
of Dionysiou, Mount Athos, Greece.

CHAPTER 6

On the Honourable Veneration of the Holy Relics

INQUIRER: What do the Holy Relics represent?

ELDER CLEOPA: The Holy Relics are miracle-working relics of certain saints. We honour them as objects in which God Himself manifests all the miraculous power of His Grace. As long as the saints were on earth, they had the Grace of the Holy Spirit in abundance—and, by this Grace, they not infrequently worked miracles. This Grace also lives in their souls in heaven where they now dwell. As the saint remains close to the people who call upon him to help them by means of a miracle, so much the more does he himself maintain an especial tie with his body, which is also a habitation of the Holy Spirit, as the Apostle says: "What? Know ye not that your body is the temple of the Holy Spirit which is in you and which ye have from God, and that

1 Cor. 6:19   ye are not your own?" Holy Scripture speaks to us concerning the miracle-workings of the saints during the period of their life on earth, that they bore witness to the power dwelling within them. Many people were healed only by touching the Apostle Peter's body and handkerchief, while others were healed only by

Acts 19:11-12   being under the shadow of the Apostle Peter when he passed by.

INQ.: Naturally, I know that the saints, just like the Saviour, performed miracles while yet in this life and that their souls possessed true faith. After their deaths, however, what power did their dead bodies possess to work miracles?

EC: I mentioned to you that the bodies of faithful people are temples of the Holy Spirit Who dwells within them. Afterward, it is the Holy Spirit Himself Who works miracles through the saints—as in life, so too after death. One pledge that the bodies of the saints, even after their death, have the power from God to work miracles is given us in Holy Scripture when it relates that the relics of the Prophet Elias revived a dead man.

2 Kg. 13:21

INQ.: Some people say that the veneration of relics resembles idol worship, which is flatly forbidden by the first and second commandments of the Decalogue. "I am the Lord thy God…Thou shalt have no other gods before Me. Thou shalt not make unto thee any graven image, or any likeness of anything that is in heaven above, or that is in the earth beneath…Thou shalt not bow down thyself to them, nor worship them." The bodies that are venerated are precisely those that these commandments forbid to be venerated.

Ex. 20:2-5

Dt. 5:6-9

EC: The holy relics are neither idols nor deities, nor figures of God, and their veneration is not idol worship. For inasmuch as God has glorified them, giving them miraculous power, so too should we venerate them, for in this way we honour God Who bestowed His grace on them. Indeed, we are obliged to honour, not the bones themselves, but their divine power. We do not erect churches to the holy relics, as did the idol worshippers for different idols and deities, but in those places where holy relics are discovered, we raise churches of God to the glory of God. The first and second commandments forbid not the veneration of the holy relics but of idols, since, unlike the pagans, we do not believe that God Himself dwells in the idols.

INQ.: Nevertheless, they say that those who touch dead bodies are considered unclean for seven days. Consequently, the touching (or kissing) of relics does not bring about sanctification or spiritual increase, but rather defilement by which, even indirectly, it is in some way possible for even the Church itself to be corrupted. Here is what we are told in Holy Scripture: "He that toucheth the dead body of any man shall be unclean seven days. He shall purify himself with the water on the third day, and on the seventh day he shall be clean; but if he purify not himself the third day, then the seventh day he shall not be clean. Whosoever toucheth the dead body of any man who is dead and purifieth not himself, defileth the tabernacle of the Lord…"

Num. 19:11-13
Lev. 21:10-11
Num. 9:6-11

EC: The cadavers of the Old Testament defiled those who touched them only because they were in sin and under the curse. In spite of that, they were not wholly unclean, since the dead body of Joseph did not defile Moses when he took it with him to Egypt, and the body of Elisha the Prophet did not defile him who was placed on his tomb, but rather healed him. In the New Testament, the relics of Christians were not unclean because they were churches and habitations of the Holy Spirit and were clean from the curse that was upon them. Consequently, they do not defile those who kiss them.

Ex. 13:19

2 Kg. 13:20-21

1 Cor. 3:16-17,
6:19-20

Further, you should know that from all of the cases of avoidance of certain things that were considered unclean, a teaching was created that pertains only to the Old Testament, which in the New Testament does not have any merit. "Therefore if ye be dead with Christ from the rudiments of the world, why, as though living in the world, are ye subject to its ordinances ('touch not, taste not, handle not,' which all are to perish with the using), according to the commandments and doctrines of men?" In the Old Testament, there were also other things considered unclean, defiling man when he touched them. For example, the clothes and bed of those who had an issue of blood, or the animals that were considered unclean in the Old Testament.

Col. 2:20-22

Lev. Ch. 15

Lev. 11:24-25

INQ.: They say that it is proper for dead bodies to be buried and to decompose in the soil from which they came and not to transgress the laws of nature. For it is written: "In the sweat of thy face shalt thou eat bread 'til thou return unto the ground, for out of it wast thou taken; for dust thou art, and unto dust shalt thou return." And also: "then shall the dust return to the earth as it was, and the spirit shall return unto God who gave it." Why, then, are the bodies of saints excluded from this path and outside of the laws of nature? Whatever else they may be, they are matter.

Gen. 3:19

Ecl. 12:7

EC: Indeed, the law of corruption of dead bodies is a general law and refers chiefly to sinners. The incorruption of the bodies of the saints proves that this law, with of course exceptions that occur, concerns sinners most of all. Holy Scripture itself testifies to us that there existed exceptions from this law and that God, for various reasons, suspended its power. Thus, for example, by the will and power of God, the bodies of Enoch and Elijah the Tishbite were not buried in the ground to decompose, but were assumed into the heavens, as Holy Scripture writes: "And Enoch walked with God; and he was not, for God took him." And again it is

1 Tim. 1:9

Gen. 5:24

said: "But upon the earth was no man created like Enoch, for he was taken from the earth." The Apostle Paul says the same: "By faith Enoch was translated, that he should not see death, 'and was not found because God had translated him.'" Concerning the Prophet Elijah, it is said: "And it came to pass, as they still went on and talked (Elijah and Elisha), that, behold, there appeared a chariot of fire and horses of fire, and parted them both asunder; and Elijah went up by a whirlwind in heaven." As for Melchizedek, we have not one mention in the Bible that he was buried somewhere since he was "without father, without mother and without descent, having neither beginning of days, nor end of life."

Eclus. 49:14

Heb. 11:5

2 Kg. 2:11
Eclus. 48:12

Heb. 7:3
see Gen. 14:18

Yet, in addition to all of that, the Body of our Saviour Himself, which was wholly like unto our body except for sin, did not see corruption in the earth, but was assumed into heaven. Hence, God made and makes exceptions from the general law of nature in the bodies of the saints, since it was He Himself who gave the law of burial and decay of bodies within the earth. Wherefore, Church history is full of examples similar to those contained in Holy Scripture.[1]

Heb. 2:17

INQ.: But if dead bodies do not first dissolve in the earth, they will not be able to be resurrected. Therefore, obstructed from the process of their disintegration, the possibility of their resurrection is annulled, as St. Paul says: "But some

---

1 To this day, throughout the Orthodox Church, and most notably on the Holy Mountain of Athos in Northern Greece where thousands of precious relics are treasured, the holy remains of Saints continue to be revealed as incorrupt, wonderworking, and myrrh-bearing. To name but a few: St. Spyridon (4th c.) on the island of Corfu (Greece) who was a father at the first Oecumenical Council in 325, St. Gerasimos on the island of Cefalonia (Greece), St. Dionysios on the island of Zakynthos (Greece), St. Theonas outside of Thessaloniki (Greece), the 120 Fathers in the Kiev Caves Monastery (Ukraine), St. John Maximovitch in San Francisco (1966) and many others in whom God is continually glorified.

man will say, How are the dead raised up? And with what body do they come? Thou fool, that which thou sowest is not quickened, except it die: And that which thou sowest, thou sowest not that body that shall be, but bare grain, it may chance of wheat, or of some other grain. But God giveth it a body as it hath pleased Him, and to every seed his own body. All flesh is not the same flesh; but there is one kind of flesh of men, another flesh of beasts…So also is the resurrection of the dead: It is sown in corruption; it is raised in incorruption. It is sown in dishonour; it is raised in glory. It is sown in weakness; it is raised in power. It is sown a natural body; it is raised a spiritual body." Consequently, it is absolutely necessary for bodies to be dissolved in the earth in order to be suited for resurrection. Why are the bodies of the saints exempted from decomposition and the resurrection?

1 Cor. 15:35-38, 42-44

EC: This text is speaking about the change which all bodies must undergo in order to be able to pass from time to eternity, to be adjusted and adapted to eternity. This change happens usually with death. In spite of all that, there exist exceptions from this order of things, such as Elijah and Enoch, as you saw, who were translated in the body without passing through death. The Apostle teaches: "Behold, I show you a mystery: We shall not all sleep; but we shall be changed in a moment, in the twinkling of an eye, at the last trumpet." Thus, it appears that it is possible for the Lord to find other methods for the transformation of our bodies, without there being a need for them to pass directly through death and decay.

1 Cor. 15:51-52
1 Thess. 4:15-17

INQ.: But Father, all dead bodies must be buried, since in the Old Testament all the righteous were entombed, while some others hid their bodies precisely so that they might not be venerated. I offer as an example the body of Moses about which we read the following: "So Moses the servant of the Lord died there in the land of Moab, according to the word of the Lord. And He buried him in a valley in the land of Moab, over against Beth-peor; but no man knoweth of his sepulchre unto this day." From that time, the Jews were inclined to idol-worship and they might easily have fallen into the error of worshipping the body of Moses. Therefore, if they hid the body, perhaps they did it precisely because if they had it before their eyes they would have venerated it?

Dt. 34:5-6

EC: The bodies of the saints—like all the Christians—were entombed also in the New Testament era with only those from which miracles occurred being disinterred and shown special veneration without, of course, them being shown worship, proper only to God. By showing this honour, they did not become idolaters, for reverence and veneration is not the same thing as idol-worship. In the Old Testament, they hid the relics of Moses—and perhaps of other righteous people as well—because the Jews were in fact inclining toward idol-worship, and if they had had them close by, they would have made them into a god like the golden calf. To avoid this delusion, it was considered good to hide the relics of some saints and just men, such as Moses, for which reason likewise we know that the Archangel Michael himself sought not to leave him in the hands of the devil. From that point on, the dead body was considered as if it was unclean (since Christ had not yet come with His hallowing Grace) and the human body was still subjected to the dominion of Satan.

Ex. 32:1-35

Dt. 9:16

Jude 1:9

In spite of all that, the Jews honoured the bodies of the dead, keeping their memory with splendour. Furthermore, you should know that the Church from the first centuries honoured the relics of the Martyrs, having them gathered with great piety and care, building temples in their honour.

Later, the practice was established of placing one piece of the relics in the Holy Altar as well as the Holy Antimension,[2] something that takes place even today.

+166 AD

The epistle of the Church of Smyrna, which describes the martyrdom of its bishop, Saint Polycarp, tells us the following: "We surrounded his relics as if they were an heirloom more costly than gold and more valued than diamond stones and we placed them in the appropriate place. Here, we would be gathered with joy, and the Lord would give us the blessing of celebrating the anniversary of the day of his martyrdom and honouring his victories and other sublime spiritual struggles."[3] This indicates that the honour of the holy relics is also applied to God Whose divine power is

Ecclesiastical History, Eusebius: 4:15

These Truths We Hold, p. 72-3; St. Tikon's Monastery, South Canaan, PA. 1986

2 "In the first centuries of Christianity, the Divine Liturgy was celebrated on the tombs of the Martyrs and this was celebrated by the Bishop. Later, as the Church expanded in size and the typical Diocese with it, the Bishops of the early Church began to ordain Priests as their representatives. . . One of the vehicles by which these important ancient practices are effected today is a simple piece of cloth . . . resting always on the Holy Table of every Orthodox Church -- the *Antimension*. The word *Antimension* is a combination of the Greek and Latin which means *in place of the table*. While Holy Tables were always to be have been consecrated and relics placed inside of them, it was not always possible for the Bishop to visit each community to do so. For that reason, Bishops consecrated cloths or boards with the holy relics inserted and sent them to each community to be used in place of the consecrated Holy Table."

+407 AD

+107 AD

See:
The Place of the Holy Relics in the Orthodox Church, Blessed Justin of Serbia in *Orthodox Tradition*, Vol. VII, No. 1, p. 9

+379 AD

3 St. John Chrysostom describes poignantly the way in which the holy relics of the Saints were translated and greeted in a eulogy on St. Ignatius: "You, inhabitants of Antioch, have sent forth a bishop and received a martyr; you sent him forth with prayers, and received him back with crowns; and not only you, but all the cities which lay between. For how do you think that they behaved when they saw his remains being brought back? What pleasure was produced! How they rejoiced! With what laudations on all sides did beset the crowned one! For as with a noble athlete, who has wrestled down all his antagonists, and who comes forth with radiant glory from the arena, the spectators receive him, and do not suffer him to tread the earth, bringing him home on their shoulders and according him countless praises.... At this time the holy Martyr bestows grace to the very same cities, establishing them in piety, and from that time to this day he enriches this city." Saint Ephraim the Syrian, in speaking of the miraculous power of holy relics, relates the following concerning the holy Martyrs: "Even after death they act as if alive, healing the sick, expelling demons, and by the power of the Lord rejecting every evil influence of the demons. This is because the miraculous grace of the Holy Spirit is always present in the holy relics."

deposited in them. We honour the relics of the martyrs so as to worship Him of Whom all the martyrs were servants, just as we honour His servants because their honour passes over to the Master Himself, as indeed He has said: "He that receiveth you receiveth me."

Mat. 10:40

Treasured at Vatopedi Monastery, Mount Athos

The Incorrupt Skull and Left
Ear of Saint John Chrysostom

Icon from the Holy Monastery of Vatopedi, Mount Athos (Detail, 13th-14th century).

Christ – The Ruler of All

CHAPTER 7

On the Honourable Veneration of the Holy Icons

INQUIRER: Some Christians wonder – why do we venerate the holy icons?

Ex. 20:4
Lev. 26:1
Dt. 5:8
Acts 7

ELDER CLEOPA: Holy Scripture forbids the veneration of sculpted figures and deities. This prohibition refers to the veneration of idols. The law, however, does not forbid the veneration of certain signs and representations of God and His holy ones, since this honour does not pertain to the material from which they were constructed but rather, via the holy visage which is depicted, our thoughts ascend to God. We saw the honour that was given to the girdle and face towel of the Apostle Paul.[1] In the Old Testament, we learn of the

Ex. 25:18-22
Ex. 26:32

Ex. 40:25

two sculpted Cherubim, which were placed above the Ark of the Covenant and on the tapestry of that holy place. It was before these that they lit incense and rendered repentance. Just as we are helped by the word to ascend beyond the

---

1 "And God wrought special miracles by the hands of Paul: from his body were brought unto the sick handkerchiefs or aprons, and the diseases departed from them, and the evil spirits went out of them" (Acts 19:12).

word, so too are we led by the icons to rise above the icons. Correspondingly, just as God wants our hearing to be made holy through spiritual discourse, so too he wants our sight to be made holy via the holy icons so that, by way of these two superior senses, there enters into the soul pure thoughts.

INQ.: Some say that we should not venerate icons since God is utterly dissimilar from the icons, no matter what honour might be due the material from which the icons are constructed or the artistry with which they are adorned. The Apostle of the Lord says clearly: "For inasmuch, then, as we are the offspring of God, we ought not to think that the Godhead is like unto gold or silver or stone, graven by art and of man's devising."

Acts 17:29

EC: Here, the Apostle is not prohibiting the veneration of the holy icons, but rather the erroneous understanding of the idol worshippers who had identified God with artistically graven figures of idols, figures the Athenian gentiles believed to be gods. When the Apostle spoke on Mars Hill he wanted to show to the teachers of the Athenians that if men are descendants of God, that is, have an immaterial soul which is the image of God in us (something which they themselves believed), then from this we can infer that God Himself is also immaterial and, thus, we are related to Him. Hence, God could not be considered identical with the material of a few sculpted deities that existed in the pagan temples of Athens. He is heterogeneous before any kind of material and it is irrational for us to identify Him with any kind of statue, whatever might be the worthiness either of the material used in its construction or of the sculptor who produced it.

In Orthodoxy, we believe in the following truth: We have sanctified icons from gold, silver, etc., which were produced with skill and talent, but we never say that God is identical and in the same category with the silver of the icon which enshrines His form. We teach that there exists one God alone, while the holy icons possess an utterly different significance from that of co-identification with God or the Saint whose form they represent. If man is far more sublime than, and of another nature from, all the statues and images which represent his form, so much the more can God not be of the same nature as images of His form.

INQ.: Icons and idols are simply material objects. God, however, as the psalm says, punishes those who place their hope in them: "The idols of the nations are silver and gold, the works of the hands of men. They have a mouth but shall not speak, eyes have they and shall not see. Ears have they and shall not hear, nor is there any breath in their mouth. Let those that make them become like unto them, and all they that put their trust in them."

Ps. 134:15-18
Ps. 113:12-16

EC: This passage is referring only to idols. If the two Cherubim of the Old Testament were placed on the vault (of the tabernacle) by the determination of God Himself, it is not possible for the holy icons to be forbidden by Him. Furthermore, if they who honoured and venerated the figures of the Cherubim in the Old Testament—during a period, mind you, when idol worship was strictly forbidden by God—were not punished, then those who venerate icons will not be punished either. It is true, of course, that while the idols are dumb and ineffectual, icons have been shown to be miraculous, not infrequently inspiring astonishment throughout the world. These miracles indicate well the attitude we should have toward the holy icons.[2]

INQ.: I have heard some say that the veneration and honouring of God via one of His icons may be a pagan custom, since only the pagans made representations of God using various materials and worshipped them. The Apostle Paul says as much concerning the idol worshippers: "Professing themselves to be wise, they became fools, and changed the glory of the incorruptible God into an image made like corruptible man, and to birds and four-footed beasts and creeping things." Thus, it is irrational for us to return to the idols or some kind of neo-pagan idol worship.

Rom. 1:23

EC: In this passage, the Apostle Paul speaks concerning the idols and the delusion of the pagans as it relates to the faith of God, not in relation to the holy icons of Christians, which is something else entirely. The Christians never imagined God, as depicted in icons, as some perishable four-footed animal or bird; but on the contrary, they painted Him as He revealed Himself to man. In this way, Christians created a clear and precise conception of the incarnate God. This is the reason the icons have always been the most fitting means of deepening piety and are the "the books of the illiterate," according to the Fathers.

---

2 Such miracles have, with passing of so many centuries, become common knowledge in Orthodox countries such as Greece, Romania or Russia. However, in recent years the United States has also witnessed miracles wrought through the holy icons in such places as Chicago, Illinois, suburban Detroit, Resaca, Georgia, and northern California. Over time such icons will often acquire a particular name, such as "Our Lady of Cicero," as with the weeping icon of the Theotokos in Chicago, IL, or being a copy of an existing miraculous icon, already possess a name, such as "She Who is Quick to Hear," as with the icon in Resaca, GA.

INQ.: God did not become visible to men and therefore no one knows how He appears, nor can they paint His form in an icon or fashion a true likeness of His Countenance.[3] He Himself has said, "Thou canst not see My face, for there shall no man see Me and live." The Evangelist John says the same: "No man hath seen God at any time." Likewise, the Apostle Paul says: "...who only hath immortality, dwelling in the light which no man can approach unto, whom no man hath seen nor can see, to whom be honour and power everlasting. Amen."

Ex. 33:20

Jn. 1:18

1 Tim. 6:16

EC: It is true that no one can see God according to His essence—in other words, as spirit—invisible to the sensible eyes of man, and infinite. Yet, not only are the eyes of man insufficient, but also his mind and thought are unable to contain Him. The boundaries of His Being span infinitude. Thus, there is no question inasmuch as it is totally impossible for us to see Him in the form that He is, i.e. in His essence. The archpriests of the Jews in the Old Testament entered into the Holy of Holies once yearly. According to their tradition they would cense the holy space plentifully, for they feared that perchance they would see God and die. The three Apostles fell to the ground when Jesus revealed to them the divine brilliance of His body on Mount Tabor. The Apostle Paul fell blind to the ground when Christ appeared to Him on the road to Damascus. So, we see that the vision of God (in His essence) remains impossible for mortal and finite man.

Ex. 30:10

Lev. 16:2, 12-13

Mat. 28:4

Acts 9:3-8

See: History of the Byzantine Empire, vol. 1, A. A. Vasiliev, University of Wisconsin Press

3 These words reflect the sentiments of the iconoclasts (icon-breakers) of the eighth century: Anathema to anyone who "ventures to represent the divine image of the Logos after the incarnation with material colors . . . and the forms of the saints in lifeless pictures with material colors which are of no value." A significant factor in the rise of the iconoclasts was the influence of Muslims, who, guided by the words of the Koran, "Images are an abomination of the work of Satan" (v. 92), viewed the veneration of icons as a form of idolatry.

And yet the Old Testament, as well as sacred history, relates to us that there were appearances of God the Father, of Jesus Christ and of the Holy Spirit. Is this in contradiction to what was said previously? Not at all. If for men it is impossible to see the essence of God, it is still possible for them to see God with their sensible eyes or their intellect (νοῦς) in forms or shapes that God might will to appear to them in His Divine Energies. These appearances take place by way of the divine economy (or dispensation) so that man might not die from the vision of God. Thus, Abraham saw the Triune God in the form of three travellers under the oak of Mamre. Jacob saw Him and said, "For I have seen God face to face, and my life is preserved." Moses also saw Him in human form, conversing with Him "face to face, as a man speaketh unto his friend." He also saw Him on Mount Horeb: "and he looked and, behold, the bush burned with fire, and the bush was not consumed."

The Prophet Isaiah said that he saw Him in the following way: "Then said I, "Woe is me! For I am undone, because I am a man of unclean lips and I dwell in the midst of a people of unclean lips; for mine eyes have seen the King, the Lord of hosts." The Prophet Daniel saw Him in the form of an aged man sitting upon a magnificent throne: "I beheld till the thrones were cast down, and the Ancient of Days sat down, whose garment was white as snow and the hair of His head like the pure wool. His throne was like the fiery flame, and His wheels as burning fire."

The Prophet Amos tells us the following: "I saw the Lord standing upon the altar." God Himself informed Aaron and his sister Miriam that He would appear to some in visible form: "And He said, 'Hear now My words: If there be a prophet among you, I, the Lord, will make Myself known unto him in a vision, and will speak unto him in a dream.

Gen. 18:1-3

Gen. 32:30

Ex. 33:11

Ex. 3:2-4

Is. 6:5

Dan. 7:9-10

Amos 9:1

My servant Moses is not so . . . with Him I speak mouth to mouth, even plainly, and not in dark speeches; and the glory of the Lord shall he behold."

Furthermore, the Son of God was seen with human and most glorious form by the Prophet Daniel, the deacon Stephan, the Apostle Paul on the road to Damascus, the holy Evangelist John, and others. And finally, the Holy Spirit of God was seen, by Saint John the Forerunner during the Baptism of the Lord, in the form of a dove, as well as by the Holy Apostles on the day of Pentecost, in the form of tongues of fire.

INQ.: If icons are indeed pleasing to God and possess divine power, why is it that God does not punish those who blaspheme, desecrate, and destroy them?

EC: We must understand that the icon depicts the human form of Christ Who, as man, came and dwelt among men. God does not punish sinners and desecrators, but rather tolerates them and desires their salvation. For this reason, He affords them time to repent, leaving them in this life. Neither, furthermore, does He discipline immediately those who blaspheme or defame His Church. Moreover, those who crucified Him He did not punish immediately, trusting in their repentance.

Beyond the grave, however, the tribunal of the Future Judgement awaits us, there where each of us will be rewarded according to his deeds.

Num. 12:6-8

Dan. 7:13-15
Acts 7:55-56
Acts 9:3-5
Rev. 1:8, 1:12, 1:20
Mat. 3:16 &
Lk. 3:21-22

Acts 2:1-4

Rom. 14:10
2 Cor. 5:10
Ps. 61:11

The Largest Fragment of True Cross in Existence
Treasured at Xeropotamou Monastery on Mount Athos, Greece.

CHAPTER 8

On the Honourable Veneration of the True Cross

INQUIRER: I hear many that are astonished to learn that we venerate the True Cross. Father, what do you have to say?

ELDER CLEOPA: The True Cross was the altar upon which was offered the true sacrifice on behalf of man for all ages. Jesus was the Offering and the Offerer, the Sacrifice and the High Priest Who administered the sacrifice, granting us our salvation. Holy Scripture testifies to this: "But Christ, being come a High Priest of good things to come, by a greater and more perfect tabernacle not made with hands (that is to say, not of this building), neither by the blood of goats and calves, but by His own blood He entered in once into the Holy Place, having obtained eternal redemption for us. For if sprinkling the unclean with the blood of bulls and goats and the ashes of a heifer sanctifieth to the purifying of the flesh, how much more shall the blood of Christ, who through the eternal Spirit offered Himself without spot to God, purge your conscience from dead works to serve the living God?" Saint Cyril of Jerusalem has this to say:

Heb. 9:11-14

"The Saviour endured all of His suffering in order to reconcile by the Blood of the Cross the heavenly with the earthly. On account of sin men became adversaries of God, with the death of sinners being the result. One of two things should have happened: Either He would have, as God, executed His will leaving all to meet death or, as the lover of mankind, suspended His decision. Yet, look at the wisdom of God! He restrained His verdict and instead showed the power of His philanthropy. Crucified in the body on the Cross, Christ took upon Himself all of sin and with His death we die to sin and live unto righteousness. It was not an ordinary man who died for us. It was not an unreasoning lamb, nor an angel, but the incarnate God Himself! The iniquity of sinners was not great, that is, not as great as His righteousness and philanthropy."

In Holy Scripture, the word "cross" has a double meaning—one with spiritual meaning, which is used very rarely, and another with material meaning, which signifies that the cross consists of two nailed crossways or the shape of a right angle made of wood upon which they crucified the greatest criminals of that epoch.

The spiritual meaning of the word "cross" is explained by the following words of the Saviour: "Whosoever will come after Me, let him deny himself, and take up his cross, and follow Me" and "And he that taketh not his cross and followeth Me, is not worthy of Me."

The other meaning is used more often in Holy Scripture. It appears clearly in the follow passages: "And He, bearing His cross, went forth into a place called the Place of a Skull (which is called in the Hebrew, Golgotha)," "And as they came out, they found a man of Cyrene, Simon by name; him they compelled to bear His cross." "Now there stood by

See Col. 1:20

1 Pet. 2:24

Mk. 8:34

Mat. 10:38

Jn. 19:17

Mat. 27:32

Jn. 19:25

Mk. 15:30

See the
next chapter

Num. 21:9

Jn. 3:14-15

the Cross of Jesus His mother and His mother's sister, Mary the wife of Clopas, and Mary Magdalene." "Save thyself and come down from the cross!"

Furthermore, the sign of the cross—which is made with the hand raised to the forehead, and then to lower-centre of the chest and then to the right and left sides—also bears the name of cross. The Cross, as a means of salvation, was prefigured in the Old Testament with a brass serpent, and in the New Testament was glorified by the Saviour: "And as Moses lifted up the serpent in the wilderness, even so must the Son of Man be lifted up, that whosoever believeth in Him should not perish, but have eternal life."

INQ.: How is possible for us to honour the instrument which was the means of punishing our Saviour?

EC: Great honour is due the Holy Cross, for upon it, as if upon an altar, in His love for man, Christ has burned up our sins. The cross has exposed *our* shame and disgrace, not the Lord's. In truth, the Holy Cross proclaims Christ's unfathomable love for mankind. Hence, our thoughts about the Cross should, in part, cause us to be ashamed and ought to inspire in us repentance for our sins. It is for us to take up our cross as the Lord took up His for us and our salvation. Of course, an object that brings about the death of an important person evokes in us sadness and pain and we do not treasure it. The same, however, does not happen with the Cross of the Saviour. On the contrary, it brings forth joyfulness and regeneration. For it was not, as some say, a place of execution but rather a place of sacrifice wherein was offered the greatest and most honourable sacrifice of the ages—the Son of Man for our salvation.

INQ.: If, therefore, we must honour the Cross, is it not necessary to honour the other instruments of salvation—such as the nails, the crown of thorns, Pilate and Judas, the archpriests Ananias and Caiaphas, and the derisive soldiers—since they all played a part in the crucifixion of Christ?

EC: It is not for us to show honour to Pilate and the other murderers of our Lord since we must also take into account the intent of those who contributed to the passion and death of the Lord. Their aim was to ridicule the Lord, to disgrace and torture Him, and, finally, to kill Him so that He would cease to exist. As concerns the crown of thorns and the nails, we honour them inasmuch as they entered into the Body of the Lord. Yet, we do not honour them to the degree to which we honour the Cross since they are spoken of nowhere in Holy Scripture, neither in the Old Testament are they prefigured, as is the case with the cross. These, then, are the reasons we honour the Cross of our Lord more than the other tools of the executioners.

INQ.: If it is truly as you say, then we should honour only the actual cross upon which Christ was crucified and not the others which have been fashioned by men. These are the work of sinful men and are not sanctified and worthy of honour and veneration.

EC: Then, we should also do the same with Holy Scripture. Today, we have an incalculable number of publications of Holy Scripture which, in your opinion, we should not honour, as they have been published by sinful or even faithless printers. Only the original text would suffice in this case. This, however, is absurd for a reasoning person, as is your previously formulated opinion is irrational.

INQ.: Yet, some say that the cross should not be paraded externally. Many hang it around their neck, others outside their houses or on top of churches and others elsewhere. Should we not venerate the cross privately within us?

EC: Whoever has it in his soul and, at the same time, sees it before him, rejoices all the more. The cross, as a tangible object, supports and strengthens internally him who carries or wears it. Holy material objects always have the effect of galvanizing and invigorating our internal spiritual experiences. Feelings of piety are born and sustained, as well, from "external" celebrations, feasts, and services experienced within the spiritual life.

CHAPTER 9

On the Sign of the Cross

INQUIRER: What is the significance of the sign of the cross?

ELDER CLEOPA: The Christian who is a faithful child of the Church of Christ—at the beginning and the end of his work, when setting out to travel, when confronted with bad news or evil thoughts, and before and after eating his meals—makes the sign of the cross upon himself, acquiring thereby the immeasurable power of the True Cross upon which was shed the All-Holy Blood of Christ over and against our common enemy, the devil. Concerning this holy sign, the following has been written: "Thou hast given a sign unto them that fear Thee, that they may flee from before the face of the bow." And also: "The light of Thy countenance, O Lord, hath been signed upon us; Thou hast given gladness to my heart." We know that in our prayer, our body with all of its members should participate. Thus, our hands play an important role in the performance of this sign.

Ps. 59:4

Ps. 4:7

    Listen to some of the testimonies contained in Holy Scripture concerning the sign of the cross. Jacob (Israel) blessed the children of Joseph with his hands stretched out in the form of a cross, as it is written: "And Joseph took them both, Ephraim in his right hand toward Israel's left hand, and Manasseh in his left hand toward Israel's right hand, and brought them near unto him. And Israel stretched out his right hand and laid it upon Ephraim's head, who was younger, and his left hand upon Manasseh's head, guiding his hands wittingly; (thus placing his arms in the form of a cross) for Manasseh was the first-born. And he blessed Joseph and said. . ." Christ blessed with His hands the children and His Apostles. Concerning the blessing of children, Scripture narrates to us the following: "And He took them up in His arms, put His hands upon them, and blessed them."

Concerning the Apostles, we read the following: "And He led them out as far as to Bethany, and He lifted up His hands and blessed them." The Apostles ordained deacons, priests and bishops with prayer and the laying-on of their hands, as a result of which the mystery of ordination is called "the laying-on of hands of ordination." With prayer and the laying-on of hands upon the heads of the candidate the Apostles rendered the mystery of Chrismation, the visitation of the Holy Spirit to the baptized. The endowment of the Holy Spirit in this Holy Mystery is called the "laying-on of hands" to distinguish from the other, earlier mentioned mystery called "the laying-on of hands of ordination." From this it is seen that the body also participates in the prayer via the hands. The Apostle also gives counsel to this effect when he says, "Glorify God in your body and in your spirit, which are God's." And elsewhere, he says, "It is my will therefore that men pray everywhere, lifting up holy hands without wrath and doubting."

In the Old Testament, reference is made to prayer that is accompanied by the participation of the body, as the psalmist relates: "So shall I bless Thee in my life, and in Thy name

Gen. 48:13-15

Mk. 10:16

Lk. 24:50

Acts 6:6, 14:23
1 Tim. 5:22

Acts 9:5-6,
8:14-17

1 Cor. 6:20

1 Tim. 2:8

Ps. 62:4

Gen. 48:14

Ex. 17:11

will I lift up my hands." The sign of the cross was prefigured in the Old Testament with the blessing of Jacob, and with the extension of the hands of Moses in the battle against Amalek, to name two examples. In the New Testament, the sign of the cross is made, as is known, in the following way. We unite the three fingers (thumb and two closest fingers) of the right hand and bring them to our forehead, saying, "In the name of the Father," honouring God the Father, the Master of all. Next, in the middle to lower section of the chest we say, "and of the Son," which denotes the descent of the Son of God to earth via His conception and gestation in the spotless womb of the Theotokos (God-bearer) for our salvation. Afterward, we place our hand on our right shoulder [and finish by crossing over to our left] saying, "and of the Holy Spirit," which expresses our reconciliation and unification with God via the grace of the Holy Spirit.

Inq.: I have heard, nonetheless, that there is no need for us to make the sign of the cross with our hand. They who worship God should worship Him in spirit and not in body: according to the words of the Apostle Paul who said: "God Who made the world and all things therein, seeing that He is the Lord of Heaven and earth, dwelleth not in temples made with hands. Neither is He worshipped with men's hands, as though He needed anything, seeing He giveth to all life, and breath, and all things." And the Lord said in Samaria: "But the hour cometh and now is, when the true worshippers shall worship the Father in spirit and in truth; for the Father seeketh such to worship Him. God is a Spirit, and they that worship Him must worship Him in spirit and in truth." Accordingly, then, the worship of God must be in spirit and not in body, with the spirit and not with our hands is the sign of the cross made.

Acts 17:24-25

Jn. 4:23-24

EC: The first passage is not concerned with whether or not the sign of the cross be made with the hand. It tells us only that we should not worship God with the toil of our hands as we would someone who is our superior. God does not have need of that kind of service. Man is so small before Him that in no case whatsoever can he aid Him in anything.

The second passage concerns other, completely different matters. Specifically, it said that soon there will begin another age in which the worship of God will be true and perfect, internal and spiritual, and not as it had existed—all but conventional (external and material). As an example, there was the mandate that the worship of God be performed in a designated place (temple), i.e. Jerusalem, Mount Gerizim and by a certain race, i.e. the Jews or Samaritans. God is spirit and consequently it is not possible for Him to be confined to the walls of a particular temple or place of Jerusalem or for the worship of Him to be monopolized. He is everywhere present and thus it is impossible for His worship to be constrained by walls and boundaries. God is spirit and thus His worship is, par excellence, spiritual and esoteric, precisely that which it was not for the Samaritans and the Jews up until that time. This spiritual worship is the true veneration that befits God, and it is this that we must strive after. This does not mean, however, that the external worship will be brushed aside, but rather that the spiritual worship, which had been disdained and scorned, is now set as the base. The external worship is necessary, for our works are both spiritual and material. If there are some who seek from us only spiritual worship, why do they themselves, when in prayer, bend their knees and incline their heads, beat their breasts, raise and cross their hands, and perform other similar movements with their body? When they make the sign of the cross with their hand, indirectly they agree that the body participates

Mat. 6:5-6

in prayer. All these movements of our body during prayer are vivid indications of a religious posture and piety before God that we should attend to inwardly as well as physically. Those who oppose the sign of the cross are enemies of the Cross of Christ. The True Cross will proclaim, in advance, the Second Coming of Christ, as the Scripture says: "And then shall appear the sign of the Son of Man in heaven. And then shall all the tribes of the earth mourn, and they shall see the Son of Man coming in the clouds of heaven with power and with great glory." This "sign" is the cross, and it is the symbol of the power and the victory of Christ.

Satan hates the Cross, for it is Christ's invincible weapon through which Hades has been vanquished and "swallowed up" and through which the deceived have been led to the truth. Satan counsels his followers to blaspheme and to spurn the Cross of Christ—for, by it, his dominion has been overthrown and his power crushed.

1 Cor. 6:20

Phm. 3:18-19

Mat. 24:30

1 Cor. 1:18

CHAPTER 10

On Prayer for the Dead

INQUIRER: If the dead have been judged and their fate decided, what assistance can our prayers possibly offer?

ELDER CLEOPA: The first thing that the soul encounters after death of the body is the judgement. There exists the partial judgement and then the general (or final) judgement, which will take place at the end of the world with the common resurrection of everyone. At the partial judgement, the status of a person in this present life will be examined. If it was good, angels escort the soul to divine glory and refreshment, while if it was evil, it is seized by unclean spirits for the torments of hell. The spiritual delight and exultation to which the worthy proceed is in Holy Scripture called "the bosom of Abraham" or "Paradise," whereas the torment in which the sinners moan is called "hell." That this partial judgement happens directly after our soul's departure from its body we see in the words of the Saviour when He said to the robber, "Verily I say unto thee, today shalt thou be with Me in Paradise." Likewise, in the words of the Apostle Paul, we read: "And as it is appointed unto men once to die, but after this

Lk. 16:22
Lk. 13:43
Lk. 16:23

Lk. 23:43

Heb. 9:27

Php. 1:21
the Judgement"; and elsewhere, "For me to live is Christ, and to die is gain."[1] Among the ancient ecclesiastical writers, we remember Tertullian who spoke the following concerning the partial and general judgement: "The soul (after death), first of all, must experience the judgement of God since it was He Who was sacrificed for all humanity which He had created. And yet, the soul will also await the resurrection of the body in order to offer recompense for whatever good it did with the help of the body, if it obeyed the commandments of God." Still further, we should know this: if someone at the partial judgement is destined for the eternal torments and is a Christian and servant of Christ, he has one hope. His hope is in the intercession of living Christians who are able to pray to Christ for him to be rescued from the torments of hell or at least to find some relief from them.

INQ.: The possibility of the intervention of the living on behalf of the dead is totally excluded, for it is known that God will judge each according to his deeds, with righteousness rendering the proper reward. Justice that occurs through the intervention of others cannot be true justice. The Apostle Paul says clearly: "For we must all appear before the judgement seat of Christ, that every one may receive the things done in the body, according to what he hath done, whether

2 Cor. 5:10
it be good or bad." Similar passages we find elsewhere in Scripture, as well as in those quotations referring to the future judgement.

On Philippians,
Homily 3,
Nicene and
Post-Nicene
Fathers
1 St. John Chrysostom says concerning this passage: "For even in dying, he says, I shall not have died, for I have my life in myself. Then would they truly have slain me, if they had power through this fear to cast faith out of my soul. But as long as Christ is with me, even though death overtake me, I live. And in this present life, it is not my living, but Christ."

EC: That God will reward each according to his deeds is an undoubted fact. However, to say that the possibility of assisting the dead through the prayers of the living faithful is ruled out is foreign to the truth. If prayer for the others yields no benefit, the Apostle Paul would not have exhorted his disciple Timothy so imploringly: "I exhort therefore, first of all, that supplications, prayers, intercessions, and giving of thanks be made for all men." While the Apostle James says "Confess your faults to one another, and pray one for another, that ye may be healed. The effectual fervent prayer of a righteous man availeth much." And no less than the Apostle Paul himself asks for others to pray for him.

Consequently, if our prayers are able to benefit the living, for what reason are they powerless to benefit the dead, granted that their souls also live? God is everywhere present and hears both the prayers for the living and for the dead. In the Old Testament, there exists a clear witness concerning prayer for the dead: "it was a holy and good thought. Thereupon he made a reconciliation for the dead, that they might be delivered from sin." While the holy Prophet Baruch says the following: "O Lord Almighty, Thou God of Israel, hear now the prayers of the dead Israelites and of their children . . . Remember not the iniquities of our forefathers . . ."

Still more clearly do the prayers existing in the Holy Tradition from the first centuries of the Church speak to us, as is apparent in the contents of the Divine Liturgies. The Holy John Chrysostom relates that it was the Apostles who instituted in the Liturgy prayers for the dead:

> "Not in vain did the Apostles order that remembrance should be made of the dead in the fearful Mysteries. They know that great gain resulteth to them, great benefit; for when the whole people stands with uplifted hands, a priestly assembly, and that revered Sacrifice lies

Ps. 61:11

1 Tim. 2:1

Jas. 5:16

Eph. 6:19

2 Mac. 12:42-45

Bar. 3:4-5

On Philippians,
Homily 3,
Nicene and
Post-Nicene
Fathers, vol. 13,
p. 409

displayed, how shall we not prevail with God by our entreaties for them?"

Jer. 17:5

INQ.: In spite of all this, there exists a passage in which the Lord speaks in contradiction to the preceeding. It is as follows: "Cursed be the man that trusteth in man and maketh flesh his arm, and whose heart departeth from the Lord."

EC: This passage states that those who place their hope of salvation exclusively in the help of men and not in God are cursed and worthy of punishment. Those separated from God in their hearts, in due course await every chastisement and pitfall, not those who have their hope *additionally* in the mediation of men in the presence of God. Otherwise, we should also consider the Apostle Paul worthy of punishment for he had asked the faithful to pray to God for him, as he had himself done for others, having hope in the benefit of these entreaties. Hence, it is impossible, from the passage you have cited, to negate the possibility and necessity of our prayers on behalf of the dead, especially given that this text is referring to something else.

INQ.: Some say that prayers on behalf of the dead are superfluous and to no avail, as the word of Scripture clearly says: "For thus saith the Lord: Enter not into the house of mourning, neither go to lament nor bemoan them, for I have taken away My peace from this people. . .They shall not be buried, neither shall men lament for them, nor cut themselves nor make themselves bald for them. Neither shall men tear themselves for them in mourning to comfort them for the dead; neither shall men give them the cup of consolation to drink for their father or mother."

Jer. 16:5-7

EC: Here, we have a word concerning sinners who have been overcome by weighty sins, something which means that for the dead whose sins are few, the distribution of bread in their memory is allowed (by the law in the Old Testament). In other words, if the passage means something else (i.e. what you think it means), then the dead should not even be buried.

INQ.: How can the priest take someone out of hell through the memorial service (i.e. prayer for the dead), since it is written, "For in death there is none that is mindful of Thee, and in Hades who will confess thee?"

Ps. 6:4

EC: It is indeed possible for someone to be redeemed from perdition, but not through the purgatorial fire as the Roman Catholics contend (their offering of expiation presented for the living and the dead notwithstanding). The Lord—as ruler of the heavens, the earth, and the infernal regions—has the power to remove a soul from Hades, as Scripture testifies: "The Lord killeth and maketh alive; He bringeth down to the grave and bringeth up."

1 Sam. 2:6
(Mat. 12:32,
Rom. 14:9,
1 Cor. 15:19)

The power and sacrifice of Christ, which is offered to whosoever seeks it, is unlimited and His goodness so great that only He is able to rescind the eternal anguish of man. We know that God asks that we love our fellow man and looks on this love with joy. When we are truly praying for others, there is nothing greater than love. God hears the prayer of the Church very clearly, especially when the prayers of Christians on earth are united with the suppliant voices of angels in the heavens and that of the Lady Theotokos. The Church carries out incessant intercession for Her members. The angels and apostles, martyrs and patriarchs, and (most especially) our Lady, the Theotokos, pray for us all. And this holy union is the life of the Church. The Saviour Himself

Mk. 11:24

assures us that our prayers will not pass unnoticed, above all, those that we make from love for our neighbour. He tells us: "Therefore I say unto you, what things soever ye desire when ye pray, believe that ye receive them, and ye shall have them." Consequently, prayer for the reposed is not only a sign and strengthening of the love we share between us, but also a proof of our faith. Thus, the Saviour says, "If thou canst believe, all things are possible to him that believeth."

INQ.: Holy Scripture also says that between Hades and Paradise there exists an impassable chasm, according to the words of the Lord in the parable of the uncharitable rich man and the impoverished Lazarus. "And besides all this, between us and you there is a great gulf fixed, so that they who would pass from here to you cannot; neither can they pass to us, that would come from there." If this really is the case, how then can it be said that we can transfer from one place to the other, from the evil to the good?

EC: Between Hades and Paradise there does exist a great chasm indeed, as our Lord has told us. Yet, this chasm does not have the power to impede the mercy of our great God, Who hears our prayers for the reposed. We do not suppose, as do the Roman Catholics, that there exists a purgatorial fire, but we say that only for those who sinned very severely (or mortally[2]) and did not confess their sin is the passage from Hades to Paradise impossible. For those who sinned more lightly, this pathway is not definitely closed—given that in the future judgement, each one's place (either in heaven or in hell) will be decided definitively, since after this judgement,

---

2 *Mortal:* destructive to life; deadly; fatal; specif., exposing to or deserving spiritual death; *Mortally:* a) fatally; deadly, b) very severely, extremely.

Mk. 11:24

Mk. 9:23

Lk. 16:26

someone whose orientation was Hades can no longer pass over into Paradise. For those who sinned unto death, our prayers are completely futile: "There is a sin unto death. I do not say that he shall pray about it." However, the situation for the other souls for whom we pray, as it is our duty, is not exactly the same. The remembrance of the dead, or memorial service, is a duty—an obligation—of love, as is every prayer for others. We are "fellow citizens with the saints, and of the household of God, built upon the foundation of the apostles and prophets, Jesus Christ Himself being the chief cornerstone." It is from the midst of this "country," this "household of God," that we call upon God to forgive our brothers and sisters who have passed over to the other world.

We do not pray for those who have committed sins against the Holy Spirit, for such sins will not be forgiven, neither in this life, nor in the one to come. Rather, we pray for those to inherit eternal life, who committed lighter sins for which forgiveness—when we pray—is also possible in the other world, inasmuch as we love them to inherit eternal life. God looks down from the heavens with attentiveness upon that which springs from love, for love is in its entirety the sum of His commandments. The Apostle says that "For in that He died, He died unto sin once; but in that He liveth, He liveth unto God."

Holy Symeon of Thessalonica observes the following:

"The Divine Liturgies are of great benefit to the reposed, whereas the other things also benefit them, but to a lesser extent (since, in departing, man ceases to sin). In contrast, through the Sacrifice they commune with Christ, are filled with divine joy and grace, being saved by divine mercy from all their agony. Consequently, the dead, above all, should be commemorated during the Divine Liturgy,

1 Jn. 5:16

Eph. 2:19-20

Mat. 12:31

1 Cor. 13

Rom. 6:10

+1430 AD

and, if the means are available, alms should be given to the poor, to erect Churches and accomplish other blessed works for the succour and salvation of the dead."

And he continues elsewhere:

"The portion that is reserved in the *Proskomedia*[3] next to the Lamb for the dead as well as his remembrance during the Liturgy unite him with God and they commune to-gether invisibly. When the brethren who have departed in repentance toward the Lord are so benefitted and comforted in this way, then likewise the holy souls of the saints also rejoice over the remembrance which is made on behalf of these departed, since they have been united with Christ and have communion through the Divine Liturgy more purely and brightly. Moreover, they commune in His Gifts with Him and pray for us. For this reason, God offered this sacrifice also for the salvation and illumination of men's bodies, as well as for us to be with Him all as one, as He has promised us. Hence, the saints pray to God for those whom they commemorate or for those in whose honour they perform this sacred sacrifice, becoming mediators for them. They pray for the living on earth to commune with Christ as they themselves commune with Him in the heavens. This is why we must commemorate the reposed since love unites the living and the dead. This is why we must also remember the saints since they rejoice at becoming suppliants for us to God."

St. Symeon of Thessalonica, works, Ch. 4

Regarding the illusive purgatory of the Roman Catholics, neither evidence nor testimony exists in Holy Scripture or in the Holy Tradition to support such a teaching. Holy Scripture makes clear only two places: Paradise and hell. In the

3 The service of preparation of the holy gifts of the bread and wine before Divine Liturgy.

+356 AD

+430 AD

553 AD

Tradition of the Holy Fathers, purgatory is not accepted. For example, Saint Anthony the Great says: "It is foolishness for someone to believe that there exists a third place in the other life." While Saint Augustine writes: "There does not exist any intermediary place, for when someone is not with Christ it is impossible for him to be in any other place except with the devil." Furthermore, we know that the Fifth Ecumenical Synod of Constantinople condemned Origen, Didymus the Blind, and Evagrius Ponticus for their teaching that the future torments and punishments will have an end. If the Church had some knowledge of the existence of purgatory, would She not have then made mention of it as an exception apart from the existence of heaven and hell?

The infinite goodness of God, the prayers of the Church, and the Eucharistic Sacrifice are effectual for the salvation of men who kept in this life the rule of repentance and departed as Orthodox Christians.

INQ.: Yes, but how can the prayers of the Church help to save souls from eternal torment before the Future (or Final) Judgement?

EC: The prayers of the Church are able to help some souls to be saved after their death but before the resurrection of the body, for the torments sinners suffer after death are provisionally and not definitively existent, unlike those that will exist after the Last Judgement. Thus, the opportunity is given to the faithful of the Church, in love, to strengthen the reposed by their prayers. Alone, the dead cannot be helped; however, with the love of others, all things are possible. The torments before the Final Judgement are not as fearful or great as those that will exist afterward, for then the body will join the soul in her suffering.

INQ.: Some say that the saints and the angels pray for the reposed who have departed in the Orthodox[4] faith. How can they know such a thing?

EC: The great Apostle Paul makes clear to us that the Saviour prays for us: "Who is he that condemneth? It is Christ who died, yea rather, who is risen again, who is even at the right hand of God, who also maketh intercession for us." Yet, he also says that the Holy Spirit prays for us: "The Spirit itself also maketh intercession for us with groanings which cannot be uttered." That the saints also pray for us, read in the book of Revelation where it says: "And when He had taken the book, the four living beings and the four and twenty elders fell down before the Lamb, having every one of them harps and golden vials full of incense, which are the prayers of the saints." Still further, we see that the saints pray for us and are heard by God in other passages. Yet, not only do the saints and the angels pray for us, they also rejoice for us: "There is joy in the presence of the angels of God over one sinner that repenteth."

Rom. 8:34

Rom. 8:26

Rev. 5:8
Job 42:8
Jas. 5:16
Rev. 8:3-4

Lk. 15:10

The Mystery of the Church, W.B. Bush, Regina Orthodox Press, Salisbury, MA. 1999.

4 This word could be rendered in English as "right glory," and is contrasted with the term heterodox, or "other glory." "The glory of God inextricably fuses the revelation of God in the Old Testament with [that] of Jesus Christ in the New Testament. . . The glory surrounding the Son's coming into the world . . . provided a sign to those who loved the God of Abraham, Isaac and Jacob that there was indeed a genuine continuity with the [Old Covenant] 'Lord of Glory.'"

Icon from the Holy Monastery of St. Catherine, Mt. Sinai (12th century).

The Second Coming and Last Judgement
of our Lord and God and Saviour Jesus Christ

In the House of God

The Athonite Elders Ephraim of Philotheou (far left) and Parthenios of Agiou Pavlou (far right).

CHAPTER 11

On Divine Services and Symbols

INQUIRER: Although in contradiction with Scripture, some say that the various movements, bows, and symbols found in the services are beneficial. What are your thoughts?

ELDER CLEOPA: A symbol is a sign that represents something or is an object that symbolizes[1] something without it being the very thing in and of itself. In that which follows, I will speak about the symbolic signs which accompany our public worship and prayer.

See:
For the Life of the World,
Fr. Alexander Schmemann,
St. Vladimir Seminary Press, p. 140-2.

1 The meaning of "symbol" was disastrously "dissolved" in Latin sacramental theology from as early as the Lateran Council of 1059 where it was opposed to the term "real." Thus, today, in the minds of most western Christians, symbol does not carry with it the meaning which the Fathers of the Church took for granted. The symbol, while still a means of knowledge, ceased to be knowledge *of* and became knowledge *about* reality. Here we can do no more than provide an inadequate idea of the term's authentic meaning, while also pointing you to a study, *Sacrament and Symbol,* from which this passage is extracted: "The symbol is means of knowledge of that which cannot be known otherwise, for knowledge here depends on participation – the living encounter with and entrance into that 'epiphany' of reality which the symbol is. . . The original sin of [scholastic] theology consists . . . in the reduction of the concept of knowledge to rational or discursive knowledge, or, in other terms, in the separation of knowledge from *mysterion* . . . . knowledge and participation [becoming] two different realities, two different orders."

The *typikon* or design of divine services is a sacred symbolic reality or a series of holy symbolic signs by which are expressed the truths of the faith – a sacred event, a devout, spiritual sentiment, a disposition of reverence, a petition.

The holy symbols and signs are expressions or externalizations and amplifications of divine worship. Divine worship is not only expressed internally, but also via exoteric means. For the veneration and adoration of God to be complete, it is absolutely necessary that the body, and not only the soul, participate in divine worship. Without this, our worship is incomplete, not integrated. Likewise, it is also true that just as without the personal participation of the soul, bodily participation in worship alone has no great worth. All of the above can also be said concerning spiritual worship. If the contribution of the symbols and ceremonies (*typikon*) are completely set aside, spiritual worship is not complete, nor could it ever be complete or integrated, just as it is impossible for a soul without a body or a body without a soul to be an integral human being.

In order for us to properly respect the value of the divine services, we must know and take into account the fact that the soul accompanies the body everywhere and participates in its every condition and effort. Thus, it is in joy that man laughs; in necessity and difficulty, he cries; and in fear, he trembles and blushes. From the expression of a man's face, you can understand the different states of his soul. Holy Scripture points out this truth to us when it says, "A merry heart doeth good like a medicine, but a broken spirit drieth the bones." And elsewhere: "A man's wisdom maketh his face to shine, and the boldness of his face shall be changed." Whereas for the murderer Cain, we read: "And the Lord said unto Cain, "Why art thou wroth? And why is thy countenance fallen? If thou doest well, shall thou not be accepted? And if thou doest not well, sin lieth at the door." While our Lord says to

Pr. 17:22

Ecl. 8:1

Gen. 4:6-7

Mat. 12:34

us: "Out of the abundance of the heart the mouth speaketh." Thus, as the sign of the True Cross is necessary in the veneration and worship of God, as are also the other symbols and liturgical signs, so too a place must be allotted to the body because it also originates with God. The Apostle Paul, inspired by the Holy Spirit, tells us the following: "Ye are bought with a price. Therefore glorify God in your body and in your spirit, which are God's." And elsewhere, he says, "I beseech you therefore, brethren, by the mercies of God, that ye present your bodies a living sacrifice, holy, acceptable, unto God, which is your reasonable service." Hence, with our body must we glorify God, offering Him veneration from the entirety of our being.

INQ.: Since God is spirit, our worship of Him must be in spirit and in truth and not in signs and in symbolic movements, external or of the body. This is what the Saviour taught us: "But the hour cometh and now is, when the true worshippers shall worship the Father in spirit and in truth; for the Father seeketh such to worship Him. God is a Spirit, and they that worship Him must worship Him in spirit and in truth."

EC: Concerning this passage, I gave you sufficient explanation previously in relation to the sign of the cross.

INQ.: Yes, but there are those who allege that the body is not to be valued and, consequently, neither should the symbols, signs, and the certain liturgical movements, according to the Saviour's words: "It is the Spirit that quickeneth; the flesh profiteth nothing. The words that I speak unto you, they are spirit, and they are life." The Apostle speaks likewise: "For bodily exercises profiteth little, but godliness is profitable unto all things, having promise of the life that now is, and of that which is to come."

1 Cor. 6:20

Rom. 12:1

Jn. 2:23-24

Jn. 6:63

1 Tim 4:8

EC: The first passage of the Evangelist John does not state that symbols and liturgical actions are worthless, neither does it discredit the worth and value of the body in that which pertains to its participation in prayer. On the contrary, this passage speaks of the heavenly provisions of the Body and Blood of the Saviour Christ, the Divine Communion, which must be understood spiritually. In Holy Communion, which is offered for our salvation, man eats and drinks the very Body and Blood of the Lord under the appearance and in the form of bread and wine. Some of the priests of the time thought that Jesus was commanding them to parcel out His Body and to eat It and to drink the Blood, something which was an especially grave offence to the Jews. The Saviour, however, through His Apostle, provides an explanation.

As for the passage from Saint Paul's letter to Timothy, the Apostle is likewise addressing another completely different matter from that which you have inferred. Here, the delusion of the heretical Gnostics—who preached and practiced complete avoidance of marriage, the eating of meat, and other things—is being opposed. The Apostle is combating this delusion in saying that the complete abstention from these things is a sin since God showed and taught that they were clean. Simultaneously, he also points out that abstaining moderately from these things is good in that it prevents us from falling into weightier sins. He not only does not say that the partial abstinence of the body profits nothing, but he says the opposite. Therefore, we cannot read into this text a diatribe in favour of the suppression of liturgical actions and symbols.

INQ.: Nevertheless, it is written: "we are the Circumcision who worship God in the spirit, and rejoice in Christ Jesus, and have no confidence in the flesh." Consequently, neither should we be grounded and sustained in the bodily participation and liturgical ordering of the Divine Services of the Church.

Jn. 6:32-34

1 Cor. 7:5-9

Philp. 3:3

a Jn. 3:5
a Jn. 7:38-39
b Jer. 2:13
b Jn. 4:14
c Is. 41:17-18
e Is. 55:1
d Ezk. 36:25
d Eph. 5:26
d Heb. 10:22
e Jn. 4:14
e Rev. 22:17
f Is. 55:1
f Mat. 3:11
f Lk. 3:16
g Jn. 3:8
g 1 Cor. 12:11
h Acts 2:2
i Mat. 3:16
i Mk. 1:10
i Lk. 3:22
i Jn. 1:32
j Eph. 1:13, 4:30
j 2 Cor. 1:22
k Is. 40:11
k Mat. 10:16
l Ps. 102:5
l Is. 40:31
m Ps. 1:3
m Jer. 24:2-7
n Ps. 17:36
o Jer. 24; 2-7
p Mat. 25:33
p Mat. 26:31
p Jn. 10:11-16

EC: Here, the Apostle speaks of the great trust and value which the Jews placed in the things of the body. The most prominent of these was the circumcision of the flesh, in which they trusted and which they boasted was sufficient for salvation. The Apostle challenges their mistaken thinking, showing that Christians are not upheld by that which is unavailing and external, but rather by the worship of God in spirit (i.e. with faith, prayer, piety, virtuous struggle, etc.) which happens with the participation of the body and thus, consequently, does not exclude the liturgical, the pious deportment, and the symbols.

In addition, Holy Scripture is filled with symbolism with which the true events of salvation history are apprehended. For example, let us look at the symbols that refer to the Holy Spirit. The Holy Spirit is named water,[a] water of life,[b] water by which the drought will cease,[c] water of cleansing,[d] water mystical and effectual,[e] water offered freely,[f] spirit that bloweth where it will,[g] tongues of fire,[h] dove,[i] and seal.[j]

INQ.: Do the symbols found in Scripture refer only to God or are other things referred to as well?

EC: No, symbols are not reserved for God alone. There are many types of symbols in Holy Scripture. To give only one example, there are many symbols which refer to the faithful, such as sheep,[k] eagles,[l] fruit-bearing tree,[m] deer,[n] good figs,[o] sheep and goats.[p]

The Temptation of Christ in the Desert
during His Forty-Day Fast.

CHAPTER 12

On Fasting

INQUIRER: Some say that the great Apostle Paul conveyed a different teaching concerning fasting from that of our Saviour Christ. Can you explain this to me?

ELDER CLEOPA: Fasting, according to the testimony of Saint Basil the Great, is the oldest commandment given by God to man. This great father of the Church of Christ says:

+379 AD

Hexaemeron. Saint Basil the Great, The Nicene & Post-Nicene Fathers, 2nd Series, Vol. 8, Philip Schaff, editor

"O Man, be pious and meditate with fear on the antiquity of the fast, for as old as is the world so old is also the commandment of fasting. Indeed, this commandment was given in Paradise when God said to Adam: 'Of every tree of the garden thou mayest freely eat; but of the tree of the knowledge of good and evil, thou shalt not eat of it. For in the day that thou eatest thereof, thou shalt surely die.'"

With the word "fasting" we mean abstinence from food, but also from all evil desires, so that the Christian may communicate his prayers to God with peace and fervour, kill his evil desires, and acquire the Grace of God. The fast is a work of virtue because it bridles the desires of the flesh, strengthens the will, assists in repentance, and thus is a means of salvation.

At the same time, it is also a liturgical action, an effort that glorifies God, when it is done for Him, for it is a sacrifice which originates from our love and reverence for God. It is a means of perfection, of cutting off the inclinations of the body, a visible sign of our zeal and struggle to acquire the likeness of God and His angels who have no need of nourishment. The fast, according to Saint Symeon of Thessaloniki, "is a work of God for Whom the necessity of nourishment is non-existent."

The aim of the fast is the benefit of the body and the soul. The fast strengthens and toughens the body and cleans the soul, maintains the health of the body, and gives wings of ascent to the soul. This is why the Old Testament recommends and imposes it many times, such as in Exodus 34:28, Deuteronomy 9:18, 1 Samuel 7:6, and Joel 2:15. And Jesus, the son of Sirach, has this to say: "Be not insatiable in any dainty thing, nor too greedy for meats; for excess of meats bringeth sickness, and gluttony will turn into ill temper. By intemperance have many perished, but he that taketh heed Ecl. 37:29-31   prolongeth his life."

The Saviour Himself fasted 40 days and 40 nights in the Mat. 6:16-18   desert before He began to preach the Gospel and He Himself teaches us how to fast. He tells us that the devil cannot be Mat. 17:21 Mk. 9:29   driven out except by prayer and fasting. His Holy Apostles and Disciples also fasted, and they themselves instituted Acts 12:2-3 2 Cor. 6:5   formal fasts for Christians.

Furthermore, we see how Holy Scripture honours the fast in certain cases and events. Moses fasted forty days and forty Ex. 34:28 Dan. 9:3, 10:3   nights, with Daniel doing likewise. The fast is beneficial when the judges and magistrates sit before God in judgement of

a Joel 1:14
a Joel 2:11-12
a Jon. 3:4-7
b 2 Sam. 1:12
b Mat. 4:3
c Joel 2:12
d Mat. 9:15
d Lk. 5:33-35
e 2Sam. 12:16 e
Dan. 9:3
e Lk. 2:37
e 1 Cor. 5:7
f 1 Sam. 7:6
f Dan. 9:3-6
g Dt. 9:18
h Is. 58:6
i Ps. 34:12-13 i
Dan. 10:2-3

the people,[a] during difficulties and dangers,[b] and it is good with regards to impending peril.[c] The fast is prescribed during both advantageous times and times of persecution for the Church.[d] The fast must be accompanied by prayer,[e] by the confession of sins,[f] and by humility.[g] The fast assists in the return of the alienated to God[h] and assists in times of grief and sorrow.[i]

The Holy Fathers of the Church of Christ strenuously extol and commend the fast. Here is what Holy John Chrysostom says about the fast: "The fast tempers the volatility of the body, bridling the insatiable appetites, purifying and enlightening the soul, and raising it up high."

The fast, in practice, is of many types. In particular:

- The complete fast, when we do not eat and do not drink at all for almost an entire day.

- Fasting with uncooked foods, when we eat, privately, dry foods in the evening only (i.e. bread and water, dry fruit, fruit, etc.).

- The conventional fast, when we eat all the accustomed fasting food, abstaining from food such as meat, fish, cheese, milk, eggs, wine, and oil.

- The light fast, when we eat food, such as fish, wine, oil etc., allowed by the Church on Great Feasts which fall on days normally reserved for fasting.

Days reserved for fasting throughout the year are as follows: Wednesday and Friday, the day of The Elevation of the Holy Cross, the Beheading of the Honourable Forerunner of the Lord, John the Baptist, and the eve of the Theophany of the Lord, all of which were established from the earliest days of the Church when the catechumens were being prepared for their Baptism on the feast by fasting and prayer.

Sept. 14th

Aug. 29th

Jan. 5th

The periods of fasting established by the Church of Christ are: The Great Fast or Great Lent, being the forty days before Holy Week and Pascha; the Nativity Fast, being the forty days before Christmas; the Dormition Fast, being the fifteen days before the Feast of the Dormition of the Mother of God, celebrated on August 15th; and the Apostles' Fast, being the period between the feast of All Saints and the feast of Saints Peter and Paul on June 29th. The order by which we are to observe these four periods of fasting are outlined in the typikon of the Church of Christ.

INQ.: Father, is it not possible that this is all an exaggeration? Man is free to eat whatever food he likes, for food in and of itself does not injure or defile him. Thus, we should not make a distinction between fasting and non-fasting foods since they are all clean, as the Saviour said: "Not that which goeth into the mouth defileth a man, but that which cometh out of the mouth, this defileth a man." The Lord explains further to the Apostle Peter: "Do ye not yet understand that whatsoever entereth in at the mouth goeth into the belly, and is cast out into the drain? But those things which proceed out of the mouth come forth from the heart, and they defile the

Mat. 15:11-18   man." Consequently, there is no reason to make a distinction among foods, since neither by fasting foods are we saved, nor by non-fasting foods are we defiled or punished.

EC: It is true that man is not defiled by the food he eats, for all is clean. However, this does not mean that fasting should not exist. Previously, I established from Holy Scripture that the fast is the oldest commandment given by God to man. Next, I enumerated certain Biblical passages that witness to the law of fasting and its benefit. The aim of fasting is not only to make a distinction between certain foods, but to discipline the body and the powers of the soul in order to realize the purification from the passions. If the Holy Prophets, Apostles, and all the Saints of God were thinking as you are, they would not have fasted so often in their lives, nor would they have left teachings on fasting to their disciples.

The passages to which you made reference do not support whatsoever the abolition of fasting, but rather refer only to the practices of the Scribes and Pharisees who never ate without first washing their hands. The Saviour explains to His disciples that which they do not understand, telling them that for someone to eat with unwashed hands is not an impure action, for the impurity of man does not originate externally but rather internally, that is, from his heart. Such was often the case with the hearts of the hypocritical Scribes and Pharisees, from which sprang words of blasphemy, hate, jealousy, and revenge towards the Lord. Such words, and not unclean hands, were the cause of their defilement. Our God and Saviour, seeing, in the depths and innermost parts, this spiritual filthiness, reproved them and called them "blind." The Scribes had the need to clean their hearts of the passions and be pure before God. And although they were actually hypocrites, they appeared to the people to be zealots for their customs, such as cleaning their hands before each meal, thinking that this pleased God. This is the true meaning of the passage that you quoted to me. With the words of this passage, the Saviour is not saying to his disciples, "Do not fast any longer," nor can this even remotely be inferred, especially if we remember that the Saviour Himself, even as the only sinless One, fasted for us and our salvation forty days and forty nights.

INQ.: There is also another passage about which I have been thinking. The Apostle writes concerning the false prophets that will appear in the last times: "Now the Spirit speaketh expressly that in the latter times some shall depart from the faith, giving heed to seducing spirits and doctrines of devils, speaking lies in hypocrisy, having their conscience seared with a hot iron, forbidding to marry, and commanding to abstain from foods, which God hath created to be received with thanksgiving by those who believe and know the truth. For every creature of God is good, and nothing to be refused if it be received with thanksgiving; for it is sanctified by the Word of God and prayer . . . For bodily exercise profiteth little, but godliness is profitable unto all things, having promise of the life that now is, and of that which is to come."

1 Tim. 4:3-8

EC: Some are convinced that we should eat of all foods, at all times, without discretion. They say that we should cast off all the restrictions of the fast and make wide the road to the belly. However, we have a teaching from our Saviour Christ that the demons are not cast out except by prayer and fasting. His holy disciples and Apostles ministered to the Lord with fasting, as it is written: "As they ministered to the Lord and fasted…" and again, "And when they had fasted and prayed and laid their hands on them, they sent them away." The great Apostle Paul did not set aside the work of fasting even in the midst of his trials: "in stripes, in imprisonments, in tumults, in labours, in sleeplessness, in fasting…"

Mat. 17:21

Acts 13:1-4

2 Cor. 6:5

Thus, whom should the Christians obey? Our Saviour Christ and His Holy Apostles or he who subverts and distorts the meaning of Scripture? The passage, which came to you in your thoughts, does not assert the abolition of fasting. From a similar misreading of this passage sprang the delusion of the ancient heretics, the so-called Gnostics. The Gnostics forbade marriage and the eating of meat. These prohibitions they kept not in short stretches of time, as we do during the

2 Pet. 3:16-17

periods of the fast, but they perpetually forbade marriage so as not to propagate "matter," while meat they considered to be unclean.

INQ.: Is it possible that fasting is something neutral or negligible? In other words, that it is not a matter of being good or bad; and, therefore, by keeping the fast, that we cannot become more pleasing to God. The holy Apostle says, "But food commendeth us not to God, for neither are we the better if we eat, nor are we the worse if we eat not." "For the Kingdom of God is not food and drink, but righteousness and peace and joy in the Holy Spirit." Thus, should we not conclude that it is no sin to neglect the fast? Those who are observant do not do wrong, but neither do those who are unobservant. Likewise, if someone keeps the fast, it is not a virtue, nor are those who neglect the fast committing a sin.

EC: This is how it appears to you, my dearest to Christ; however, it is not at all like this. You say that the fast cannot make anyone acceptable before God. What did the Ninevites do in order not to be lost and to call off the just judgement of God? They fasted. Their fasting brought down God's mercy upon them and averted the destruction of the 120,000 inhabitants who had fasted together with their king and animals. Was not the Prophet King David able to appease God with his prayer and fasting after his fall into debauchery and murder? Listen to what he says: "I ate ashes like bread," and elsewhere he says, "But as for me, when they troubled me, I put on sackcloth. And I humbled my soul with fasting, and my prayer shall return to my bosom." Did not the fast of the three youths, who were cast into the fire without being burned, please God? Did not the Prophet Daniel close with fasting the mouths of lions in the den? Let these testimonies

1 Cor. 8:8

Rom. 14:17

Jon. 3-4

Ps. 101:10

Ps. 34:15-16

Dan. 1:8-15
Dan. 3:25
Dan. 6:23-24

suffice, for here there is not room to show you how many other people pleased God through fasting.

Besides this, you should know that the two passages you cited do not at all refer to fasting, but to the sacrifices of food offered by the idol worshippers, as is apparent from the text of the two passages. Examine the above passages and you will see that those who were scandalized by the sacrifices of food offered to idols were judaizing Christians who kept with great accuracy the laws of the Old Testament pertaining to the handling of food. They did not eat the meat from the sacrifices and wanted to prohibit those Christians who came from among the Gentiles from doing so. With this pretext, the Apostle Paul wrote the above passages.

INQ.: Father, in our thoughts, perhaps we should remain far from such matters, as the Apostle Paul says: "Let not him that eateth despise him that eateth not; and let not him that eateth not, judge him that eateth; for God hath received him. Who art thou who judgest another man's servant . . . He that eateth, eateth to the Lord, for he giveth God thanks; and he that eateth not, to the Lord he eateth not and giveth God thanks;" and "Let no man therefore judge you in meat or drink, or in respect to a holy day or the new moon or the Sabbath days, which are a shadow of things to come, but the body is of Christ."

EC: The first passage, like those to which you made an appeal earlier, does not forbid or abolish the fast. The Apostle is referring only to the distinction made between foods forbidden and allowed or between clean and unclean food, according to the old order of the Old Testament. In the second passage cited, he is countering the judaizing Christians who accused certain Christians coming from the Gentiles of eating the

1 Cor. 8:10,

10:25-27

Dt. 14

Rom. 14:3-6

Col. 2:16-17

meat of animals offered to idols. The Apostle shows that the actions of the Gentile Christians have no implication for their salvation. From this dispute arose the opportunity to put an end to the unrest, disorder, and disagreement that had appeared between the Jewish and Gentile Christians as concerned, particularly, the handling of food and, generally, the problem of the obligations of Christians to the Mosaic Law. The text gives ample explanation as to the nature of the problem. If you read the Holy Scripture with care, with the help of the patristic commentaries, you will understand the text clearly and will not be led astray into error. However, if you only read one passage or one text and give rest to your thoughts falling into agreement with a few others, then little by little delusion overtakes you.

INQ.: Some believe that the true fast is only the so-called "black fast," which consists of total abstention for a designated length of time from every type of food and drink. This fast should be assumed, however, with a free will, according to the abilities and conditions of each, and never on defined days or in determined periods of the year.

EC: Neither does our Church condemn the "black fast." On the contrary, it commends it, for it has a Biblical basis. Yet, this fast may be very difficult, and not everyone is able to practice it due to differences in the health and temperament of the body. For this reason, the Church ordained another, more lenient type of fast, that also has Biblical basis, to be obligatory for each Christian.

INQ.: How, then, are we to observe the true fast according to the teaching of the Orthodox Church?

EC: The true fast, my brother, must be observed not only with the body, but also with the soul. In other words, we do not only eat fasting foods but we abstain from the passions, temptations, and sin. When we abstain from lush and pleasurable food, we struggle to purify not only the body but also the soul by means of prayer and repentance. The complete, true, and perfect fast is not only of the body, but also of the soul.

We are taught this in the *troparion* (hymn) which we chant during Great Lent: "Let us keep the acceptable fast, that which is pleasing to the Lord." The true fast is the estrangement from evil, the bridling of the tongue, the negation of wrath, the turning away from lust, hate, deceit, lies, and from all untruthfulness.

Let us end our discussion on this subject with the teaching of Holy John Chrysostom:

> "Dost thou fast? Give me proof of it by thy works! Is it said 'By what kind of works?' If thou seest a poor man, take pity on him! If thou seest an enemy, be reconciled to him! If thou seest a friend gaining honour, envy him not. If thou seest a beautiful woman, pass her by! For let not the mouth only fast, but also the eye, and the ear, and the feet, and the hands, and all the members of our bodies. Let the hands fast, by being pure from pillaging and avarice. Let the feet fast, by ceasing from running to the hateful theatres and along the pathways of sin. Let the eyes fast, being taught never to fix themselves rudely upon handsome countenances, or to busy themselves with strange beauties. For looking is the food of the eyes, but if [looking] be such as is unlawful or forbidden, it

The Homilies on the Statues to the People of Antioch, Homily 3, number 11, The Nicene and Post-Nicene Fathers, First Series, Vol. 9, Phillip Schaff, editor

mars the fast and upsets the whole safety of the soul; but if it be lawful and safe, it adorns fasting. For it would be among things the most absurd to abstain from lawful food because of the fast, but with the eyes to touch even what is forbidden. Dost thou not eat flesh? Feed not upon lasciviousness by means of the eyes. Let the ear fast also. The fasting of the ear consists in refusing to receive evil speaking and calumnies. Let the mouth, too, fast from disgraceful speeches and railing."

The Ladder of Divine Ascent

The twelfth-century icon illustrating St. John Climacus' classic book (of the same name) in which is described the path and process of salvation.

CHAPTER 13

On the Presuppositions of our Personal Salvation

INQUIRER: Father, earlier you spoke about our "personal salvation." Can you tell me more about this?

ELDER CLEOPA: Some religious confessions teach that personal salvation presupposes the action of Divine Grace alone, according to Calvin, or the grace of faith—i.e. of trust in God—according to Luther, by which the "merits" or virtues of our Lord Jesus Christ are conferred upon man. Therefore, to give a general outline, there are Protestant Christians who believe that salvation stems only from faith and that on the part of man himself there is placed no condition or requirement for his salvation.

Our Church, however, teaches that our personal salvation is neither a gift, nor a simple work, but rather a process and an undertaking that matures or develops gradually and is realized in the co-operation of two persons: God and man. On the part of God, Divine Grace (His uncreated Divine Energy) is offered to us, while, for man's part, faith and righteous deeds are necessary. Consequently, the prerequisites for our personal salvation are the following: the Divine Grace or uncreated Divine Energy of God and the faith and virtuous deeds of man.

Our objective salvation is realized only in the sacrifice of Jesus Christ, whereas our personal or subjective salvation, which in the language of the New Testament is called "righteousness," "holiness," or "salvation" (in the narrow sense), is realized as a continuance of this objective salvation, with our personal energy or activity acting in co-operation with Divine Energy or Grace.

On the part of God, Divine Grace is absolutely necessary, for we "all have sinned and fallen short of the glory of God," and we are justified by His grace, redeemed in Christ Jesus. "For it is God who worketh in you, both to will and to do of His good pleasure." "For by grace are ye saved through faith, and not that of yourselves: it is the gift of God—not by works, lest any man should boast. For we are His workmanship, created in Christ Jesus unto good works, which God hath beforehand ordained, that we should walk in them."

From this, it is clear that divine Grace is necessary for our personal salvation. This truth is also evident in the words of the Lord: "I am the vine, ye are the branches: He that abideth in me, and I in him, the same bringeth forth much fruit: for without me ye can do nothing. If a man abide not in me, he is cast forth as a branch, and is withered; and men gather them, and cast them into the fire, and they are burned. If ye abide in me, and my words abide in you, ye shall ask what ye will, and it shall be done unto you."

Hence, the Grace of God is for us the fluid that runs from the vine to the vine branch. On the part of man, saving and actualized faith is necessary—that is, "faith which worketh by love." Without man contributing this, salvation is not held out for him. Conscious faith in God, without good deeds, the demons also possess, for they too "believe and tremble."

Rom. 3:23-24

Philp. 2:13

Eph. 2:8-10

Jn. 15:5-7

Gal. 5:6

Jas. 2:19
Mat. 25:34
Jn. 5:29
Rom. 2:6-13
2 Cor. 5:10 Jas.
2:14-26 Rev.
20:12 and others

Holy Scripture itself makes clear that good works are necessary for salvation. Holy Scripture is filled with passages that refer to good deeds as a necessary prerequisite of our salvation.

INQ: I have gathered from different discussions I have had with representatives of various confessions that they are of the opinion that divine Grace operates by force and irresistibly. For them, it is not possible to speak at all of freedom, nor of a certain worthiness of man in whatever pertains to his salvation. It is said that this is apparent from the parable of the Lord: "And the Lord said unto the servant, go out into the highways and hedges, and compel them to come in, that my house may be filled." Elsewhere the Lord also said: "No man can come to me, except the Father which hath sent me draw him: and I will raise him up at the last day." It is claimed that with this meaning in mind the Apostle Paul says the following: "For it is God which worketh in you both to will and to do of his good pleasure." It would seem clear from all of these citations that there does not, in fact, exist freedom of will and that God alone, independent of our disposition, grants salvation.

Lk. 14:23

Jn. 6:44

Phil. 2:13

EC: Holy Scripture teaches us clearly that man is created by God free and self-governing, that is, with freedom of will, as the Holy Spirit tells us: "O Lord as with a shield of Thy good pleasure hast thou crowned us." Elsewhere it says, "He Himself made man from the beginning, and left him in the hand of his counsel," and again, "He hath set fire and water before thee: stretch forth thy hand unto whichever thou wilt." Furthermore, in another place in Holy Scripture it is said: "Behold, I set before you this day a blessing and a curse; a

Ps. 5:13

Eclus. 15:14

Eclus. 15:16

blessing if ye obey the commandments of the LORD your

Dt. 11:26-27

God..." And further on it is said: "See, I have set before thee this day life and death, good and evil . . . I call heaven and earth to record this day against you, that I have set before you life and death, blessing and cursing: therefore choose

Dt. 30:15, 19

life, that both thou and thy seed may live."

The freedom of the will of man, as well as the dependence of salvation upon his freedom, appears more clearly from the words of the Saviour Himself: "O Jerusalem, Jerusalem, thou that killest the prophets, and stonest them which are sent unto thee, how often would I have gathered thy children to-

Mat. 23:37
Lk. 11:20
Mat. 19:17
Heb. 4:11
Rom. 2:4

gether, even as a hen gathereth her chickens under her wings, and ye would not!" Whereas to the rich young man He said, "If thou wilt enter into Life, keep the commandments."

Through the mouth of His prophet Isaiah, God says the following: "If ye be willing and obedient, ye shall eat the good of the land. But if ye refuse and rebel, ye shall be devoured

Is. 1: 19-20

with the sword." And again, to the rich young man He says, "If thou wilt be perfect, go and sell that thou hast, and give to the poor, and thou shalt have treasure in heaven: and come

Mat. 19:21

and follow me."

In all of these passages, it is positively obvious that God fashioned man with freedom of will and does not compel the will of anyone to draw near to salvation. For if the will of man is coerced into accepting salvation, then any compensation in the future life would be meaningless. Likewise, God would cease to be the just judge whom the Holy Scriptures custom-arily refer to Him as being. If our salvation is accomplished without our personal will, then that which the great Apostle Paul says would be incomprehensible to us: "For we must all appear before the judgement seat of Christ; that every one may receive the things done in his body, according to that he

2 Cor. 5:10

hath done, whether it be good or bad." And likewise, "Now

1 Cor. 3:8

he that planteth and he that watereth are one: and every man shall receive his own reward according to his own labour."

INQ.: Fair enough, but I still have serious doubts. Is it not possible that God, from before the ages, determined the fate of each one of us? In other words, some are to be saved and some to be punished, analogous with the decisions rendered from time immemorial, out of His sovereign pre-ordination for each one of us? The following words of the Apostle Paul appear to support this opinion.

"For the children being not yet born, neither having done any good or evil, that the purpose of God according to election might stand, not of works, but of him that calleth; It was said unto her, The elder shall serve the younger. As it is written, Jacob have I loved, but Esau have I hated. What shall we say then? Is there unrighteousness with God? God forbid. For he saith to Moses, I will have mercy on whom I will have mercy, and I will have compassion on whom I will have compassion. So then it is not of him that willeth, nor of him that runneth, but of God that sheweth mercy. For the scripture saith unto Pharaoh, Even for this same purpose have I raised thee up, that I might shew my power in thee, and that my name might be declared throughout all the earth. Therefore hath he mercy on whom he will have mercy, and whom he will he hardeneth. Thou wilt say then unto me, Why doth he yet find fault? For who hath resisted his will? Nay but, O man, who art thou that repliest against God? Shall the thing formed say to him that formed it, Why hast thou made me thus? Hath not the potter power over the clay, of the same lump to make one vessel unto honour, and another unto dishonour?"

Rom. 9:11-21

The same Apostle says elsewhere,

> "Blessed be the God and Father of our Lord Jesus Christ, who hath blessed us with all spiritual blessings in heavenly places in Christ: According as he hath chosen us in him before the foundation of the world, that we should be holy and without blame before him in love: Having predestined us unto the adoption of children by Jesus Christ to himself, according to the good pleasure of his will."

Eph. 1:3-4

From this, it seems evident that salvation is offered according to the decision of God from before the ages. For the Apostle says likewise elsewhere: "But we are bound to give thanks always to God for you, brethren beloved of the Lord, because God hath from the beginning chosen you to salvation through sanctification of the Spirit and belief of the truth: Whereunto he called you by our gospel, to the obtaining of the glory of our Lord Jesus Christ." Furthermore, the following is written in another passage: "But we speak the wisdom of God in a mystery, even the hidden wisdom, which God ordained before the world unto our glory." And elsewhere, it is said: "what hast thou that thou didst not receive? Now if thou didst receive it, why dost thou glory, as if thou hadst not received it?" "For it is God which worketh in you both to will and to do of his good pleasure." Hence, consequently, the problem is posited as follows: No one is saved except those who were pre-elected and predestined by God from before the ages. Man, in this life, follows the lot prescribed for him by God without the possibility of changing or replacing it.

2 Thess. 2:13-14

1 Cor. 2:7

1 Cor. 4:7

Phil. 2:13

Life of Moses, Book II, paragraph 11, Saint Gregory of Nyssa

EC: Holy Scripture contains within it unanswerable passages or, as Saint Gregory of Nyssa puts it, "strong bones." Some would like to break these bones of Scripture with their wisdom teeth, as of yet still only suitable for sucking milk. However, such a thing they would never be able to manage. All who have desired to plunge into the depths of Scripture have drowned in the fathomless ocean that is the wisdom of God. Such was the portion shared by Origen, Arius, Macedonius, Nestorius, Sabellius, Dioscorus, Eutyches, and all the other chiefs of the ancient heresies who have been swallowed up in the unfathomable sea of Holy Scripture. The profundity and depth of Scripture was not the cause of their fall and drowning, but rather they themselves were the cause, due to their own insufficiencies, of being drowned in the depths of the mysteries of the Scriptures.

Holy Scripture is like a fountain or an endless spring of the wisdom of God in which we must be steeped and partake in accordance with our level of wisdom and spiritual maturity. Just as we take water from the well with a bucket, empty it into our pitcher, and then into our glass in order to quench our body's thirst, so must we also do with our spiritual thirst when we are urged to drink of the deepest ocean of wisdom, the Holy Scriptures. Thus, spiritually speaking, if we draw more water from the well of Scripture than is drinkable (out of desire for the purity of our intellect [νοῦς] and heart), due to our pride and inquisitiveness, we will be destroyed in our attempt to grasp the incomprehensible with our limited human faculties. If, for example, we were to see a child from the first grade trying to learn and to teach others that which is taught at the university, how much laughter and amusement would it provoke in us! The same and worse happens to those who desire to scrutinize and unravel the incomprehensible mysteries of the Scriptures with an intellect inexperienced and unenlightened by the Holy Spirit.

The divine Prophets and Apostles, as well as the holy Fathers of the Church, while, by the purity of their lives, attained to the simplicity and innocence of infants—at the same time also, on account of their wisdom—became as "perfect spiritual men." Nevertheless, they were never so bold as to delve into the impenetrable mysteries of the wisdom of God. Before these elevated notions and expressions, they remained as if enraptured saying, "How great are Thy works, O Lord, exceeding deep are Thy thoughts," and "Great is our Lord, and great is His strength, and of His understanding there is no measure." Still further, in another place, it is said: "Hast thou not known? Hast thou not heard, that the everlasting God, the Lord, the Creator of the ends of the earth, fainteth not, neither is weary? There is no searching of his understanding." Listen also to the vessel of election, the Apostle Paul, as he says with wonderment; "O the depth of the riches both of the wisdom and knowledge of God! How unsearchable are his judgements, and his ways past finding out! For who hath known the mind of the Lord? Or who hath been his counsellor?"

You [should] understand, therefore, my friend, that this fathomless depth of the wisdom of God cannot be approached by any intellect among His creatures, neither those found in the heavens, nor those on earth. Much more difficult is it for those who, without purifying their intellect (νούς) and heart from the passions, and being bereft also of divine enlightenment, presume on their own to penetrate the unbounded abyss of the Scriptures.

My dearest to Christ, earlier you referred me to certain passages that appeared to you to underscore a type of absolute predestination for man. However, the truth of things is entirely otherwise.

The first passage refers to the call of man toward the grace and righteousness which is in Christ Jesus. The Apostle desires with this example to illustrate that the call and right-

Marginal references: Eph. 4:13 · Ps. 91:6 · Ps. 146:5 · Is. 40:28 · Rom. 11:33-34 · Rom. 9:11-21

see above
Rom. 9:22-24

eousness of men do not depend on the "works of the law" but on the goodness of God Who calls by His Grace all men to salvation, both Jews and Gentiles. Without the grace of God, men are powerless to accomplish anything with regards to their salvation. Here the Apostles is underscoring the importance of the presupposition of our objective salvation or sanctification (i.e. the salvation of the race of man collectively), without repeating again the personal presupposition: the freedom of man in co-operation with the grace of God, with faith and good works.

Furthermore, in no sense is it maintained that the foreknowledge of God exists as a basis for the predetermination of the soul or the predestination of each one of us. This is unstated yet implicit when the Apostle says that there are those whom God chastens and hardens since they had become "instruments of wrath," God tolerating them with forbearance. God perceives everything in advance and is not dependent upon the passing of time to know that between the two sons of Isaac one would be the conveyor of His messianic promise. Thus, it is nothing to marvel at when He says: "Jacob I have loved, but Esau I have hated."

If it is said that God has mercy on whomever He wishes and punishes whomsoever He wishes, then we must ask: Upon whom does God want to show mercy and upon whom does He desire to inflict punishment? If He loves him that He has predetermined for salvation, who in this life would be evil? Likewise, if He punishes those who reject Him, who in this life would be good? Or does God want certain among the good to become evil and certain among the evil to become good without any righteous judgement or requital? Yet, in this case, where is righteousness? Where is equity or impartiality? Where is wisdom and all of the other attributes of God? Not even among men is it possible for such things to occur, and yet even when men are given over to arbitrariness it is a tragedy and setback.

As for the other passages you cited, they do not refer to some type of categorical predestination of the eternal life of the soul, but rather to the election or call of the soul to the Christ-sent grace. The call or election of the soul is not based on its worth or virtue but rather solely on the goodness of God. This invitation is not expressed and offered to a few, as is maintained by the followers of unqualified predestination, but rather to every human being, since the Apostle is speaking only in the plural and thereby showing that it is not that some are preferred and especially invited in the sense of predestination.

It is with this understanding that the Apostle Paul says: "For this is good and acceptable in the sight of God our Saviour, Who will have all men to be saved, and to come unto the knowledge of the truth. For there is one God, and one mediator between God and men, the man Christ Jesus; Who gave himself as a ransom for all, to be testified in due time." If from this text we wanted to expound an unconditional predestination for the heavenly majesty, a predestination of this sort would have to be understood according to the letter and spirit of the text, i.e. as unrestricted and unbounded. However, this would mean that salvation comes automatically to everyone, and it is well known that it does not. Furthermore, the very followers of predestination themselves maintain that the number of the predestined for salvation is restricted.

1 Tim. 2:3-6

The truth is that Christ has brought salvation to everyone, something theologians have labelled general (or objective) salvation. And yet, not everyone actualizes this objective salvation, only those who seek and pursue it. While objective salvation is granted to every human being, subjective or personal salvation depends on the intent of man. Those who desire to be saved and work toward that goal receive divine Grace as their aide and guide. This Grace does not work in us violently; rather, it abides with us perennially as a specific offering for the work of our salvation. Subsequently, it is not possible for us to speak of an unconditional predestination and its inadequate presuppositions for salvation. The truth concerning the predestination, fate, and life of man can be summed up as follows.

A) Holy Scripture speaks often of a kind of predestination that carries with it the meaning of *pre-knowledge*. At times it is spoken of directly, being referred to variously as "foreknowledge" and "predestination," "the counsel of His will," "the mystery which hath been hid from the ages," and the "book of life."

Acts 2:23
Rom. 8:29
Eph. 1:11
Col. 1:26
Eph. 3:9
Rev. 20:15
Lk. 10:20

This predetermination is based on the life and works of man, which are plainly evident to our All-knowing God. Indeed, Holy Scripture speaks precisely: "And we know that all things work together for good to them that love God, to them who are called according to his purpose. For those whom he foreknew, he also predestined to be conformed to the image of his Son, that he might be the first-born among many brethren. Moreover those whom he predestined, them he also called: and whom he called, them he also justified: and whom he justified, them he also glorified."

Rom. 8:28-30

We know also that, at the future judgement, there will be specific criteria upon which all will be judged. No one will be judged arbitrarily for that judgement will be righteous and unprejudiced. The Apostle says, "For we must all appear before the judgement seat of Christ; that everyone may receive the things done in his body, according to what he hath done, whether it be good or bad." And, "But this I

Mat. 25:34-36

2 Cor. 5:10
1 Cor. 3:8

2 Cor. 9:6
say, he which soweth sparingly shall reap also sparingly; and he which soweth bountifully shall reap also bountifully."

Furthermore, Holy Scripture sets forth this teaching with more clarity in other ways. It is often repeated that God does 2 Pet. 3:9
Eph. 4:6
Rom. 3:29

Mat. 28:19
Rom. 10:18 not want the death of any sinner, that He is "not willing that any should perish," that all are called to salvation, and that God gave His grace to overflowing, precisely there where sin abounded, in order to provide all men with the possibility of salvation. All of this would be made a lie if the number of the chosen were in fact limited.

B) History certifies with all of the Church Fathers and theologians of great authority, together with the entirety of Holy Tradition and its incontestable substantiating elements, that the teaching on divine foreknowledge has always existed within the Church.

+202 AD
- Saint Irenaeus says: "God, who knows everything, has made ready the proper dwelling: for to those who seek after and yearn for the unapproachable light; God in His goodness grants them that light."

+407 AD
- Saint John Chrysostom says: "God has not foreordained us for salvation only out of love, but also on account of our good deeds, because if this (salvation) were dependent only upon our good works, then the coming of Christ and everything which He has effected for our salvation would be as though it were unnecessary."

+367 AD
- Saint Hilary writes similarly: "That which God foresaw, He also foreordained."

+420 AD
- Blessed Jerome writes: "For that which God knew would happen in the life of His Son, that He also permitted (pre-ordained) for His Son."

+397 AD

- Saint Ambrose says: "God did not predetermine without seeing first that which He foreknew. Likewise, in those whom He foresaw worthiness, to those He also preordained a spiritual reward."

Inq · If grace is always necessary for salvation, whatever the case, and if salvation is a gift of God given with grace, do we have a part in the working out of our salvation?

EC: Yes, we certainly do have a part to play, but grace is also necessary for our salvation, for man cannot be saved on his own. We are not like logs or stones with which God does whatever He likes.

If grace were to work on its own—indifferent to us—it would mean that we would walk to our salvation without our will. In this case, if some are lost to perdition, they would not be to blame, but rather grace would be responsible, since it did not compel them to be saved. This teaching, as we have said previously, is not a teaching of Christ's Church but of the Calvinists who have themselves termed it unconditional election or predestination. According to this teaching, God decided from before the ages to save certain men and destroy others. This He does in accord with His liking, not according to the way man would work, but through His grace—grace that He decided to give in order to save some. To a few, grace is given—grace that compels them to work according to His will—while from others, grace is withheld. Such is the teaching of the Calvinists.

Inq.: And the teaching of the Orthodox Church is different from that?

EC: Previously, I showed you the Church's teaching clearly enough and at quite some length, and yet I will add for you

1 Tim. 2:4   also the following: "God our Saviour will have all men to be saved, and to come unto the knowledge of the truth." Grace does not compel anyone. Men have the God-given freedom to accept it and to work with it or to reject it. Those who embrace it are saved and those who withdraw from it are lost. Guard well, my son, that which you have heard, that you may be illumined by it and believe as a true Orthodox Christian.

Icon from the Holy Monastery of Vatopedi, Mount Athos (13th century).

Jesus Christ the Saviour of the World

"Come unto Me, all ye that labor and
are heavy laden, and I will give you rest."

Icon from the Monastery of Saint Catherine, Mount Sinai (12th century).

Moses Receiving the Ten Commandments

CHAPTER 14

On Keeping the Lord's Feast on Sunday Instead of Saturday

INQUIRER: If the New Covenant is a continuation of the Old Covenant, how is it that we don't commemorate the seventh day (Saturday) as a Feast day.

ELDER CLEOPA: From Adam until the death of Abraham, according to certain chronologies, 3,678 years passed, to which must be added the 403 years in which the Jews were captive in Egypt, totalling 4,108 years. During the period from Adam until Moses, neither were the Scriptures written nor Saturday observed as a Feast day by any race of people. For so many thousands of years, the patriarchs and faithful of God were guided along the path of salvation only by the Holy Tradition. Finally, after so long a time, while the Israelites were passing through the desert of Arabia, God at last blessed the Sabbath day. He blessed the Sabbath day, in commemoration of the creation of the world in seven days (on the seventh day on which God rested), and of the exodus of His people from the slavery of Egypt. Holy Scripture recounts these events as follows: "And God blessed the seventh day, and sanctified it: because that in it he had rested from all his work which God

Chronology of George Kedrinos

Gen. 2:3

created and made." Elsewhere, in reference to the exodus of the Israelites from Egypt, it is written: "And remember that thou wast a servant in the land of Egypt, and that the LORD thy God brought thee out thence through a mighty hand and by a stretched out arm: therefore the LORD thy God commanded thee to keep the Sabbath day."

Dt. 5:15

Yet, nevertheless, it should be well understood that the Sabbath was not given by God as an obligatory Feast for all the people of the world, but was sanctioned as a Feast and eternal agreement only for His people Israel. Holy Scripture makes this clear: "Wherefore the children of Israel shall keep the Sabbath, to observe the Sabbath throughout their generations, for a perpetual covenant. It is a sign between me and the children of Israel forever: for in six days the LORD made heaven and earth, and on the seventh day he rested, and was refreshed."

Ex. 31:16-17

In another passage, Holy Scripture shows us also that the Sabbath and all of the other commandments of the Law were given to Israel alone: "He declareth His word unto Jacob, His statutes and judgements to Israel. He hath not dealt so with every nation, nor hath He shown His judgements unto them." In other words, to the unbelieving nations that did not descend from the race of Jacob, with its commandments, God did not appear. One of these commandments included the commandment concerning the Sabbath. When the idol-worshippers came to Nehemiah wanting to take part in the building of the temple, he told them: "The God of heaven, He will prosper us; therefore, we His servants will arise and build: but ye have no portion, nor right, nor memorial, in Jerusalem." If the idol-worshippers had kept the Sabbath, would Nehemiah have had the right to speak to them in that way? The idol-worshippers could have answered him that they, too, have the Sabbath as a sign of a covenant

Ps. 147:8-9

Neh. 2:20

with God, just like the Israelites. To the contrary, however, Nehemiah states clearly and firmly that they have no place or right in Jerusalem.

As a further testimony that neither the Law nor the Sabbath was given to the idol-worshippers, we have the epistle of Saint Paul to the Romans, where he says, ". . . when the Gentiles, which have not the law, do by nature the things contained in the law . . ." And further on, the same Apostle says that to the Israelites "pertaineth the adoption, and the glory, and the covenants, and the giving of the law, and the service of God, and the promises."

Rom. 2:14

Rom. 9:4

With the above examples as a base, one comes easily to the conclusion that the command to keep the Sabbath was a sign of union and covenant between God and Israel—that, consequently, it was given only to the people of Israel, and not to all men without distinction.

Ex. 3:16-17

And yet, neither was the commandment of the Sabbath given for an indiscriminate amount of time. The Apostle Paul in his epistle to the Galatians shows us that "it was added because of transgressions, till the seed should come to whom the promise was made; and it was ordained by angels in the hand of a mediator." Moreover, we know that "Christ is the end of the law."[1] Behold, then, for what duration of time the Law was intended: until the coming of the end which is Christ Himself. The Law, as we know, was for

Gal. 3:19

Rom. 10:4

Discourse on the Nativity of the Most Holy Mother of God, Saint Andrew, Archbishop of Crete (+720 AD)

1 "Here is the end (of the law): the Lawgiver, having made everything, hath changed the writing into spirit and doth head everything within Himself (Eph 1:10). For the lawgiver hath taken the law under His dominion, and the law is become subjected to grace. The Lawgiver's aim is not that the properties of the law suffer reciprocal commingling, but only suchlike, that the servile and subservient (in the law) by Divine power be transmuted into the light and free (in grace), 'so that we' — sayeth the Apostle — 'be not enslaved to the elements of the world' (Gal 4:3) and be not in a condition under the slavish yoke of the writing of the law. Here is the summit of Christ's beneficence towards us! Here are the mysteries of revelation! Here is the *theosis* [deification] assumed upon humankind — the fruition worked out by the God-man."

Christ only pedagogical, in order that we might be justified by faith. After the coming of faith, we are no longer under the "schoolmaster" of the Law, for the Old Testament was replaced, fulfilling the command of Jeremiah, in which he says: "Behold, the days come, saith the Lord, when I will make a new covenant with the house of Israel and with the house of Judah: Not according to the covenant that I made with their fathers in the day when I took them by the hand to lead them out of the land of Egypt. . . For this is the covenant that I will make with the house of Israel after those days, saith the Lord; I will put my laws into their mind, and write them in their hearts: and I will be to them a God, and they shall be to me a people." Here, the prophet speaks of the closing of one covenant and refers to the time in which this covenant will be replaced with a new one. Yet, this begs the question: what covenant will be replaced? The Prophet Jeremiah offers us the following: "Behold, the days come, saith the LORD, that I will make a new covenant with the house of Israel, and with the house of Judah: Not according to the covenant that I made with their fathers in the day that I took them by the hand to bring them out of the land of Egypt; which my covenant they brake."

In what exactly this covenant consists, the Prophet Moses informs us: "The LORD our God made a covenant with us in Horeb. The LORD made not this covenant with our fathers, but with us, even us, who are all of us here alive this day . . . I stood between the LORD and you at that time . . . These words the LORD spake unto all your assembly in the mount out of the midst of the fire, of the cloud, and of the thick darkness, with a great voice: and he added no more. And he wrote them in two tables of stone, and delivered them unto me."

Gal. 3:24-25

Heb. 8:8-10
Jer. 31:31

Jer. 31-32

Dt. 5:2-22

This covenant, this concord, must be replaced with the New Covenant. Consequently, inasmuch as this old accord has been replaced or fulfilled, so too has the command to keep the Sabbath.

INQ.: But father, our Christ has not dissolved the Law of the Old Testament, for He Himself said: "Think not that I am come to destroy the Law or the prophets: I am not come to destroy, but to fulfil. For verily I say unto you, Till heaven and earth pass, one jot or one tittle shall in no wise pass from the Law, till all be fulfilled." Does this not seem to imply that the Sabbath would also remain valid forever?

Mat. 5:17-18

EC: Christ did not dissolve the Law and the Prophets, or in general the Old Testament; He only replaced it with the New Covenant, which is more complete than the Old. The Old Testament, as is apparent above, has only an instructive character, with the aim of preparing mankind for the coming of the Saviour: "Wherefore the law was our schoolmaster to bring us unto Christ, that we might be justified by faith. But after that faith is come, we are no longer under a schoolmaster." Our salvation no longer hangs on the performance of the mandated works of the Old Testament or on the observing of the Sabbath, but on our faith in Jesus Christ, our Saviour. Through Jesus Christ, the old Law was fulfilled and ceased to exist, "for Christ is the end of the law for righteousness to every one that believeth." The old Law was observed up to the time of Saint John the Baptist, who was also the last to prepare the way for the coming of Christ. Those who are under the authority of the law have been born under the mastership of slavery, exactly as the son of Abraham who descended from his father's slave, Hagar. Those living under the Law of Grace can be likened to the son of Abraham that

Gal. 3:24-25

Rom. 10:4

Mat. 11:13

Gal. 4:22-31
was born of his free wife, Sarah, inasmuch as they are born for freedom and an inheritance. Hence it is that Hagar and Sarah are representative of the two Covenants. And thus it is also that the words of the Saviour, "Think not that I am come to destroy the law, or the prophets," have the following meaning: I did not come contrary to the Law and the prophets, or, My coming is not something strange, but on the contrary, it is towards the fulfillment both of the Law of Moses as well as all the books of the prophets. In this way, Rom. 10:4 with My coming I fulfill the Law perfectly, since it was for this reason that I came.

When the Saviour says that "till heaven and earth pass, one jot or one tittle shall in no wise pass from the law, till all be fulfilled," He is referring to the realization of the words of the prophets concerning Him. These prophecies found their fulfillment precisely in that offering of His own blood at the Mystical Supper, from which the accord of the Old Testament also found its end. Having eaten with His disciples, the Saviour took the cup and gave it to them saying, Lk. 22:20 "This cup is the new testament in my blood, which is shed for you."

Inq.: In spite of this, it is also true that God blessed and sanctified the seventh day even from the creation of the world and the completion of His work, as it is written: "And on the seventh day God ended his work which he had made; and he rested on the seventh day from all his work which he had made. And God blessed the seventh day, and sanctified Gen. 2:2-3 it: because that in it he had rested from all his work which God created and made." Consequently, after the six days of creation, the seventh day was the first Sabbath that was made holy by God Himself, and due to this fact, should it not remain holy for all people and all ages?

EC: These two passages speak only of God and His work, saying that God finished His work, rested, blessed, and hallowed the seventh day. They do not, however, say anything concerning man, nor would it have been possible for man to have a day of rest only one day after his creation. Placed by God "into the Garden of Eden to dress it and to keep it," the first man did not receive any command with reference to observing the seventh day as a feast or day of rest. The only command that God gave him was to not eat of the fruit of the knowledge of good and evil. For man, all the days were of the same rank. Even more so, of course, was it the case that they received no command to observe a particular day festively after Adam and Eve transgressed the commandment, knew good and evil, and were thrown out of Paradise. On the contrary, the entire life of man is one continual workday, since he is bound to labour all his days on the earth, safeguarding his food—for, as it is written, "in sorrow shalt thou eat of it all the days of thy life."

Gen. 1:26-31

Gen. 2:15

Gen. 2:16-17

Gen. 3:17

It is apparent, indeed, that God rested on the seventh day of His work, but as to what this day was called we are not informed. By implication, then, the following questions arise:

- Is the seventh day, in fact, the same as the Sabbath?

- Were the days of the week then numbered in such a way that the seventh day corresponds to the contemporary Saturday or Sabbath?

- Where is it related that, in fact, the days were numbered and how were these days called in those days?

- And, at the very least, can you show me where exactly the word "Sabbath"—about which you have spoken with someone so exhaustively—is written?

It is true, indeed, that God rested and sanctified the seventh day, but what does the seventh day actually signify? Nowhere are we ever told that for this day there was "the evening and the morning" as we are told concerning the other days of creation. If this were the case, God would have continued on the eighth day—the first day of the next week—to begin to create the world again or to do work of some sort because, after the sixth day, He would have to rest once again. Furthermore, for God Himself, the seventh day of each week would be a feast and day of rest. This would mean that the feast day of the Sabbath would be a day of rest according to the example of God alone, without being based on a particular commandment from the beginning. The commandment, however, came much later.

The seventh day is nothing more than the day on which God ceased from his work of creating the universe. Nowhere in Holy Scripture are we told that, from the beginning, man also ceased from his work on the seventh day.

INQ.: There exists a passage in which we can see that the command to sanctify the seventh day was not given in the time of Moses' sojourn in the desert, but that it existed even from the creation of the world: "Remember the Sabbath day, to keep it holy." You see here that God draws the attention of our intellect to this already existing commandment—a command that was not instituted at this point for the first time. And since it existed from the beginning, it means that all people, of every age, and not just those who came after Moses, must observe it.

Ex. 20:8

EC: "Remember" refers to that which exists from before (i.e. "remember" something that I said some other time). For, indeed, the command to keep the feast of the Sabbath was not given for the first time on the same date with the other commandments on Mount Sinai. Yet, it is not as it appears to you, dearest to Christ, that it was given in the beginning to Adam in Paradise. This commandment was assuredly given later on and for the first time in the desert of Sinai, when God, through Moses, charged the Jews not to gather manna on the Sabbath or seventh day. It is for this reason that the first commandment starts with the words, "Remember the Sabbath day": in order to remind the Jews that He had given them this commandment earlier than the others. Thus, the Sabbath did not originate in Paradise, nor was this feast celebrated until the days of Moses.

Ex. 16:25

INQ.: Is it possible for the feast of the Sabbath to have been replaced, since it is a sign and eternal agreement between God and men, having as its basis the words of God Himself? "Wherefore the children of Israel shall keep the Sabbath, to observe the Sabbath throughout their generations, for a perpetual covenant. It is a sign between me and the children of Israel for ever." Thus, the substitution of the Sabbath with Sunday or with any other day would mean the substitution of an eternal covenant with a human one.

Ex. 31:16-17

EC: It is true that the Sabbath is an eternal covenant that was given by God, however, not for all the peoples of the world, but only for the people of Israel. This fact we can better understand from the testimonies of Holy Scripture.

First of all, we see that the Lord spoke to Moses and said for the descendants of Israel to keep the Sabbath as a day of rest from generation to generation, as an eternal covenant. In a second passage, this covenant is a commemoration of the enslavement in the land of Egypt from which God had freed the Israelites, charging them, as a memorial, to keep

Ex. 31:16

the Sabbath as a day of rest: "And remember that thou wast a servant in the land of Egypt, and that the LORD thy God brought thee out thence through a mighty hand and by a stretched out arm: therefore the LORD thy God commanded thee to keep the Sabbath day." And thirdly, we see that the Sabbath is a visible sign between God and the children of Israel. "And the LORD spake unto Moses, saying, 'Speak thou also unto the children of Israel, saying, Verily my Sabbaths ye shall keep: for it is a sign between you and me throughout your generations; that ye may know that I am the LORD that doth sanctify you." The Prophet Ezekiel expresses this in the same way: "Thus saith the Lord GOD . . . I gave them my Sabbaths, to be a sign between me and them, that they might know that I am the LORD that sanctify them." And fourthly, it is apparent that the Sabbath and the entire Law was given only to the Hebrews, and not for the other peoples and nations. This is derived from the testimonies of the rulers of the chosen people who returned from exile. For, when foreigners came and sought from them permission to help in the building of the temple, they said to the Jews: "Let us build with you: for we seek your God, as ye do; and we do sacrifice unto him since the days of Esarhaddon king of Assyria . . ." In response to these words, the envoy of the Gentiles explicitly and categorically received the following answer on behalf of Nehemiah: "The God of heaven, he will prosper us; therefore we his servants will arise and build: but ye have no portion, nor right, nor memorial, in Jerusalem."

Take especial note of the second to last word, "memorial." This word is repeated sometimes by God and other times by Moses in order to draw our attention to the feast of the Sabbath or to the covenant (given through Moses) between God and His people who were saved from the slavery of Egypt. It is said, "Remember the Sabbath day," and "remember

Dt. 5:15

Ex. 31:12-13

Ezk. 20:5, 12

Ezra 4:2

Neh. 2:20

Ex. 20:8

Dt. 5:15

that thou wast a servant in the land of Egypt . . . therefore the LORD thy God commanded thee to keep the Sabbath day." Subsequently, this commemoration refers to the agreement-covenant of the Sabbath which God contracted with the Israelite people when He led them out of the bondage of Egypt. The other nations do not have this covenant of the Sabbath because they never had any covenant with God, as did the Hebraic people—and, thus, they have no reason to commemorate this feast of the Sabbath.

Ezra 4:2

After the Hebrews were carried away into Babylonian captivity, the peoples that gathered in Palestine and possessed the land mixed with the remaining Hebrews and believed in their God. This faith, however, was not able to make them participants in the history of the chosen people and its covenant with God concerning the Sabbath. For this reason, they were repelled from the building of the temple, being told that they did not have a "memorial in Jerusalem." In other words, the Sabbath is an exclusively Jewish feast and cannot be transferred to other peoples, even if they believe in the God of Israel. This is a truth that cannot be misinterpreted and which all those keeping the Sabbath must clearly understand, for it pertains to the Old and New Testament.

If this covenant of the Sabbath is referred to as being "eternal," the word "eternal" here must be understood by us as having the meaning of a particular stability that cannot be changed or substituted by men. By no means, however, can we suppose that God does not have the power to alter or replace it, given the fact that, as we know, the Saviour Himself transformed this "eternal" covenant of the Sabbath. Therefore, the word "eternal" here means the epoch of the Old Testament, at the end of which began a new age and a new covenant, the covenant given as a promise even in the Old Testament. Yet, the word "eternal" is used in the Old

Testament on other occasions as well—as, for example, in the command to keep the feast of the paschal lamb, for which God charges the Hebrews: "ye shall keep it a feast to the LORD throughout your generations." The same applies to the feast of Unleavened Bread, which He charges them to keep, it being an eternal covenant. Besides all of this, those who today observe the Sabbath do not also keep the feast of the paschal lamb according to the Old Testament traditions—the rubrics with unleavened bread and the bitter herbs, loins girded, shoes on the feet, with staff in hand and in haste, ready to leave. The "eternal law" is also the undying flame of the oil lamp hanging before the veil of the ark of the Law in the temple of Jerusalem. The ritual of the slaughtering of animals for the sacrifice is also called an "eternal covenant." In spite of all this, those who keep the "eternal" covenant of the Sabbath do not honour these other "eternal" laws and covenants, for then they would have to return to all of the rubrics and rituals of the Old Testament.

INQ.: Another, similar scriptural testimony was produced for me in which it is shown that the observance of the feast of the Sabbath is required of all Christians of all races and peoples. Hence, the Saviour "came to Nazareth, where He had been brought up: and, as His custom was, He went into the synagogue on the Sabbath day, and stood up for to read."

Furthermore, it is written of the Apostle of the nations that "Paul, as his manner was, went in unto them (i.e. into the synagogue of the Jews of Thessaloniki), and three Sabbath days reasoned with them out of the scriptures." And, elsewhere, it is written: "The women also, which came with him from Galilee, followed after, and beheld the sepulchre . . . And they returned, and prepared spices and ointments; and rested the Sabbath day according to the commandment."

Ex. 12:14

Ex. 12:17

Ex. 12:1, 24

Ex. 27:20-21
Lev. 17:7

Lk. 4:16

Acts 17:2

Lk. 23:55-56

So, it seems that they also honoured the commandment of the Law and kept the Sabbath day. And the Saviour, speaking about the end of the world, revealed that the Sabbath will remain until the end, saying, "Pray ye that your flight be not in the winter, neither on the Sabbath day." Whereas the Apostle Paul, speaking of the Sabbath day's repose, says that God gave to His people "rest." His people are Christians from all nations and all ages. Is it not they, therefore, that are required to keep the rest of the Sabbath?

Mat. 24:20

Heb. 4:4-11

EC: We no longer have any need of keeping the Sabbath. The New Testament has succeeded the Old, dedicating another day to rest and celebration—the first day of the week,[2] the Lord's Day. The consecration of this day of celebration and rest is independent of the old Sabbath. The Sabbath of the old Law, as we showed earlier, was instituted by God as a day of celebration and rest in memory of the exodus from the slavery of Egypt of only one people: the people of Israel. On Sunday[3], however, we celebrate the memory (ἀνάμνησις[4])

The Bible and the Liturgy, J. Danielou

[2] The first day of the week is also known as the eighth day: "The number eight was, for ancient Christianity, the symbol of the Resurrection, for it was on the day after the Sabbath, and so the eighth day, that Christ rose from the tomb. Furthermore, the seven days of the week are the image of the time of this world, and the eighth of life everlasting. Sunday is the liturgical commemoration of the eighth day, at the same time a memorial of the Resurrection and a prophecy of the world to come. . ." And elsewhere we are reminded that Sunday represents ". . .an eighth and eternal day, consecrated by the Resurrection of Christ . . . There we shall rest and see, see and love, love and praise."

City of God, bk. 22, ch. 30, St. Augustine

[3] In Greek the word for Sunday (Κυριακή) comes from the word for Lord (Κύριος), and could literally be translated as "the Lord's day."

The Worshipping Church, Fr. George Florovsky Introduction to *The Festal Menaion,* pg. 28, St. Tikhon's Seminary Press

[4] "The Christian remembrance (*anamnesis*) is much more than just a memory or reminiscence. ... The individual events of the past (Incarnation, Cross and Resurrection, Pentecost) are, at the same time, paradoxically present in the Church here and now. The Incarnation of the Word is at once an historic event of the past which can and should be 'remembered' in the ordinary way, and also an *abiding presence* of the Lord which can be directly perceived and recognized . . . by the eye of faith, in the Church. ... The accomplishment of the Promise was not just an extra event in the homogeneous sequence of happenings. It was an 'event' indeed, but it was an event which *never passes.*"

of the resurrection of the Lord, through which was accomplished the renewal and regeneration of the entire world, our exodus from the slavery of sin and the acquisition of the heavenly Canaan.

The teaching on the abolition of the Sabbath in the New Testament is supported both on an indirect (particular and general) and direct basis (from the life of Christ and the Apostles).

The New Testament "made old" its predecessor, thereafter called "Old," and fulfilled all of the old agreements (laws), among which belonged also that of the Sabbath. The Old Testament was not complete, but rather it was—at the very most—a shadow, a figure. Observe, then, why a new testament had to have been founded. In saying "new covenant," the Lord made old the first, which existed only in the "time of reformation," that is, until it was reformed and perfected by the New Law. "For if that first covenant had been faultless, then should no place have been sought for the second." Thanks to the second Covenant, all things in the Old Testament, "behold, . . . have become new." Once and for all, the ordinances of the Old Law have been annulled and replaced, including the feast of the Sabbath. Having all of this in mind, the great Apostle Paul writes against those who would want to practice the ordinances of the old Law and criticize those who do not observe them, giving correction with the following words: "Let no man therefore judge you in meat and drink, or in respect to a holy day or the new moon or the Sabbath days, which are a shadow of things to come, but the body is of Christ."

It is true that those who would acquire salvation must be descendants of Abraham. Descendants of Abraham, however, are not those who are descendants according to the flesh, but those that place their faith in the fulfilment of the

Heb. 10:1
Col. 2:16-17
Heb. 8:5-8

Heb. 8:13

Heb. 9:10, 10:9

Heb. 8:7

2 Cor. 5:17

Rom. 7:1-6

Col. 2:16-17

Messianic promises. These descendants of Abraham, then, are Christians, who become children of God and free from the ineffectual injunctions of the law—dictates that Christ, with His gospel commandments, has blotted out, as they are an obstacle to our salvation. "[He has] blotted out the handwriting of ordinances that was against us, which was contrary to us." Salvation does not come from the works of the law, but from our faith in Jesus Christ, for "the just shall live by faith." Christians, therefore, must show the proper veneration due to the Old Testament, but in no case should we honour it more than the New Testament or even to the New Testament's detriment.

Our Saviour Jesus Christ, who did not come to abolish the Law and the Prophets but to fulfill them, observed all of the commandments of the Law, excepting only one—that of the Sabbath. For if He went to the synagogue as every Jew did on the Sabbath, it was with the aim of preaching to the people gathered there or to heal the sick, and not that He might be an example for us to observe the Sabbath. The Jews then, as they still do today, had the habit of gathering at the synagogue on Friday evening for prayer. If our Saviour also went on this day to the synagogue, would this then mean that we should also keep a memorial on Friday as well?

I see that you have the thought that Christ and the Apostles had regard for the Sabbath. Truly, but what kind of recognition was this? It is known only that He performed a majority of His miracles on the Sabbath, something for which they threatened Him with death. The following were healed on the Sabbath: the man with the withered hand, the woman bowed down with a spirit of infirmity, the man with dropsy, the man with an unclean spirit, the man with an infirmity for thirty-eight years, the man born blind. Three of these restorations to health—of the man with the withered hand,

Gal. 3:5

Col. 2:14

Rom. 1:17

Mat. 5:17

Jn. 5:16

Mat. 12:9-14

Lk. 13:10-17

Lk. 14:1-6

Mk. 1:21-26

Jn. 5:1-18

Jn. 9:1-18

the hunched-over woman, and the man with the unclean spirit—not only happened on the Sabbath but in the hall of the synagogue itself.

Concerning the passage, "Pray ye that your flight be not in the winter, neither on the Sabbath day," it is good to remember that here the text is not speaking of the sanctification or veneration of the Sabbath. Saint Ephraim the Syrian, a great teacher of the truth, explains that the word "winter" signifies that we not be seized by God in the winter of our unpreparedness, while the word "Sabbath" signifies that we not be overcome by heresies. With these words, the Lord does not *forbid* us the Sabbath rest, since He Himself made *allowance* for it, saying, "The Sabbath was made for man, and not man for the Sabbath: Therefore the Son of man is Lord also of the Sabbath." But, neither did the Apostles respect the day of the Sabbath, for they plucked and ate ears of corn, even though it was the Sabbath. The holy Gospel tells us, in addition, that the Jews sought to kill Jesus "because He not only had broken the Sabbath, but said also that God was His Father." Christ, however, as Lord also of the Sabbath, reproached it: "Having abolished in his flesh the enmity, even the law of commandments contained in ordinances." The Saviour made a new covenant by His blood and, through the example of His life and work, instructed us to no longer keep the day of the Sabbath as a religious observance. And if our Jesus Christ taught us this with His words and actions, is it possible for us to ignore Him—He Whom we have "put on" and in Whose Name we have been baptized?

You have also referred to the fact that the holy Myrrh-bearers kept and honoured the Sabbath day "and rested on the Sabbath day according to the commandment." Indeed, the Myrrh-bearers, as the simple women that they were, honoured the Law and all its prophets. They followed Christ,

Mat. 24:20

Mk. 2:27-28

Mat. 12:1-3

Jn. 5:18

Eph. 2:15

Lk. 22:20

Gal. 3:27

Lk. 23:55-56

but—like Joseph of Arimathea, who the holy Gospel says was a council member and "a good and just man"—they kept to the Law out of fear of the Jews. Joseph of Arimathea, "a rich man" and "an honourable council member," while in such fear of the Jews that he followed Christ secretly, out in the open worked as every Jew, even taking part in the council. How much more, then, would a few women fear not keeping the Sabbath in violation of the Law?

Lk. 23:50

Mat. 27:57

Mk. 15:43

If we carefully examine the New Testament, we see that all of the commandments of the Decalogue—in their substance—proceed from the Saviour or the holy Apostles, except for the commandment of the Sabbath. The first commandment we find in Matthew 12, verses 31 to 32, and in Mark 3, verse 29. The second commandment we find in St. Paul's first letter to the Corinthians, chapter 10, verse 14, and 1 John 5, verse 21. The third commandment is found in James 4, verse 12, and chapter 5, verse 12. The fifth commandment is found in Matthew 15, verses 4 and 19. The sixth is found in Matthew 19, verse 18, and Mark 10, verse 19. The seventh, eighth and ninth commandments are found in Matthew 19, verse 18, in Mark 19, verse 10, and in the letter to the Romans, chapter 13, verse 9. And the tenth commandment we find in Romans 13, verse 9.

Yet, in spite of all this, nowhere in the Gospel or the epistles of the Apostles do we find even an allusion made to the fourth commandment, the commandment concerning the Sabbath day. This should make it clear to us that this commandment no longer exists for the Saviour and the Apostles. And if it no longer exists, then   naturally—neither is it spoken of any longer. Our Saviour Jesus Christ condensed all the commandments into two, in love of God and love of our neighbour, saying, "On these two commandments hang all the Law and the Prophets." Likewise, the Apostle teaches us that love is the totality of the law.

Mat. 22:40

INQ.: Nevertheless, it is claimed that the Apostles and early Christians observed the Sabbath and that it was only from the time of Constantine the Great in 321 that the innovation of celebrating the feast on Sunday was introduced, thereafter becoming obligatory.

EC: It is not true that the Apostles and the first Christians kept the Sabbath. If the great Apostle Paul went to the synagogue on the Sabbath, he did not go in order to be observant of the Sabbath, but because it was there that the Jews were all gathered together and there that he had the opportunity to speak to them from the Scriptures. The Apostle Paul did not speak to the masses only in the synagogue, but in the marketplaces and houses, and even outside of the gates of the cities in the fields. He did not only speak to the people on the Sabbath, but all day and all night. And what kind of rest did the Apostle Paul enjoy on the day of the Sabbath? He toiled working in the field of the souls of men in the service of the word of God.

Jn. 18:20

Acts 17:2

Acts 17:7

Acts 16:13

Acts 20:31

Acts 6:2

The Apostles were not alone in not giving special honour to the Sabbath—their successors did likewise: Barnabas, Ignatius the God-bearer, Polycarp of Smyrna, Clement of Rome, Justin Martyr, Tertullian, and many others of the first, second and third centuries. They confess that the Christians of their epoch celebrated with exactness the feast of Sunday— the Lord's day—following, as we know from Scripture, the Apostles in this practice.

Concerning Constantine the Great, history testifies only to the fact that during the time of his rule Christianity was recognized as a free religion by the state. This recognition subsequently supported the spread of Christianity throughout the Roman world, as well as the observance of the religious duties of Christians, among which was the holy day and feast of the Lord, Sunday. Thus, the Roman State did nothing else except recognize and sanction a practice already in existence.

INQ.: What are the Scriptural foundations for keeping the Lord's feast on Sunday instead of Saturday?

EC: For believing Christians, the greatest feast is the Resurrection of Christ—the day of joy—for on this day, Christ Himself greeted the Myrrh-bearing women, saying: "Rejoice!" The day of Resurrection is the day on which our Saviour Jesus Christ freed us from the slavery to sin, just as He once freed His chosen people from the bondage of Egypt. The day of Resurrection is a day sanctified with His priceless Blood. It is a day of declaration that we have risen from the death of sin and that we will rise also from the bodily death unto an eternal life—if, that is, we die with steadfast faith in Christ, as the Apostle Paul says: "And if Christ be not raised, your faith is vain; ye are yet in your sins. Then they also which are fallen asleep in Christ are perished." And in another passage: "And if Christ be not risen, then is our preaching vain, and your faith is also vain."

Therefore, according to the witness of the Apostle Paul, the faith of a Christian is worth nothing without complete trust that Christ has risen from the grave on the third day as He Himself foretold. If the Resurrection of Christ is so important for each Christian, should he not always have it in mind and honour it, celebrating the "putting on" [of Christ] with white garments of purity and virtue, like the angels who rolled back the stone from the tomb?

The Lord's day (Sunday), the day of our salvation, is also called in Holy Scripture "the first day of the week," "after eight days," or "the day of the Lord." The three days of which

Mat. 28:9
1 Pet. 2:24

1 Cor. 15:16-17

1 Cor. 15:14

Mat. 28:3

Mk. 16:2
Jn. 20:26
Rev. 1:10

Holy Scripture speaks are the days in which the Saviour remained in the tomb, the number of which was also typified in Holy Scripture with the Prophet Jonah and his stay within the belly of the whale for three days. This number likewise corresponds to the number of days in which the Saviour said He would raise the temple of God. And that which He had said by way of the prophets to His disciples, that He would rise from the tomb on the third day, the Saviour brought to pass with His Resurrection. On the first day of the week, the event of His Resurrection took place; and on the first day of the week, in Emmaus, He performed the first Liturgy with the breaking of the bread before His two disciples. It was on the evening of the first day of the week, "when the doors were shut where the disciples were assembled for fear of the Jews, Jesus came and stood in the midst of His disciples and said unto them, "Peace be unto you." It was on the first day of the week (Sunday) that the Saviour breathed on His disciples giving them the power to bind and to loose the sins of men. On the same day of the week, as well, He appeared to His disciples again, with Thomas present, for whom He fortified his faith in His Resurrection. In addition, it was on Sunday that He appeared in Galilee. And it was on this day that the Apostles celebrated the breaking of bread, in other words, the Divine Liturgy. On the same day, the gathering of economic aid and preaching as organized by the Apostles took place in order to assist the impoverished Christians.

Thus it is then, that the same resurrectional day, as a day of the glory of the Lord, became also the feast of the love of the brethren. Of this day, the psalmist speaks when saying, "This is the day which the Lord hath made; let us rejoice and be glad therein." And likewise, it was on the Lord's day that the Revelation revealed to the Evangelist John came to pass.

Mat. 12:40

Jn. 2:19-22

Mk. 16:9
Mat. 28:1-10

Lk. 24:30

Jn. 20:19-20

Jn. 20:26

Acts 2:1-10

Acts 20:7-12

1 Cor. 16:1-2

Ps. 117:24

Rev. 1:10

INQ.: Are there other ancient testimonies that during the first centuries the early Christians celebrated the feast on the Lord's day (Sunday)?

EC: I believe I have referred you to a sufficient number of testimonies concerning the feast of Sunday from both Holy Scripture and the Christians of the ancient and contemporary Church, as well as for what reason they kept the feast of Sunday instead of Saturday. You should also know that, besides those contained in Holy Scripture presented previously, there are many other trustworthy testimonies from the holy Apostolic Fathers, the disciples of the holy Apostles who were their successors and who personally heard their words.

+107 AD

One of these was Saint Ignatius the God-bearer, bishop of Antioch. In the epistle that he sent to the Christians of Magnesia, he says the following:

The Epistle to the Magnesians, ch. 9, The Ante-Nicene Fathers, Vol. 1, Edited by A. Roberts & J Donaldson

"Those who were brought up in the ancient order of things have come to the possession of a new hope, no longer observing the Sabbath, but living in the observance of the Lord's Day, on which also our life has sprung up again, by Him and by His death."

Later, writing in the second century after Christ, St. Justin the Martyr writes:

+155 AD
First Apology, chapter 67, The Ante-Nicene Fathers, Vol. 1, Edited by A. Roberts & J Donaldson

"Sunday is the day on which we all hold our common assembly, because it is the first day on which God, having wrought a change in the darkness and matter, made the world; and Jesus Christ our Saviour on the same day rose from the dead."

Bk. 2, Ch. 59

In addition, we find similar testimonies in the *Didache* (or Teaching of the Twelve Apostles), in the canons, and the multitude of the holy Fathers and writers of the Church from the second to the fourth century—as for example, in Tertullian, Saint Irenaeus, Saint Ambrose of Milan, Saint John Chrysostom, and many others.

It was for this reason, then, that with the sanctioning of Sunday as a day of rest for the entire empire—including even non-Christians—by the Emperor Constantine the Great, it has remained even until today a weekly day of rest for all Christian peoples.

See also 29th Canon of the Synod of Laodicea, 364 AD

Icon from the Catacombs of St. Peter and Marcellinus.

The Healing of the Woman with an Issue of Blood

Mosaic from the Church of Osios David, Thessalonica (5th century).

Christ in the Glory of His Second Coming

"And he who sat upon the throne said, 'Behold, I make all things new.' ... And he said to me, 'It is done! I am the Alpha and the Omega, the beginning and the end. ... I am the root and the offspring of David, the bright morning star.' The Spirit and the Bride say, 'Come.' And let him who hears say, 'Come.' ... And let him who is thirsty come, let him who desires take the water of life without price.' ... And he who testifies to these things says, 'Surely I am coming quickly.' Amen. Even so, come Lord Jesus!"

CHAPTER 15

On the Second Coming of Christ

INQUIRER: Father, what can you tell us about the exact date of the Second Coming of Christ?

ELDER CLEOPA: Christ's true Church provides us with a number of apt testimonies which show that God did not entrust this date to anyone, neither to angels, nor to men, nor even to His own Son as man.

Listen to the divine words of Scripture on the subject:

> "But of that day and hour knoweth no man, no, not the angels of heaven, but my Father only. But as the days of Noe were, so shall also the coming of the Son of man be. For as in the days that were before the flood they were eating and drinking, marrying and giving in marriage, until the day that Noe entered into the ark, and knew not until the flood came, and took them all away; so shall also the coming of the Son of man be . . . Watch therefore: for ye know not what hour your Lord doth come. But know this, that if the goodman of the house had known in what watch the thief would come, he would have watched, and would not have suffered his house to

Mat. 24:36-51

be broken up. Therefore be ye also ready: for in such an hour as ye think not the Son of man cometh . . . ”

If neither the angels in heaven nor the Son of Man Himself as man know the appointed time, how is it possible for it to be known among men? From the words of the Saviour, it is only understood that we must be ever vigilant and mindful of our salvation, ever ready for the coming of the Lord, for we know neither the day nor the hour of His coming, nor even the hour of our own end in this life. His appearance will be unexpected, as the Lord forewarned us when he said, “Watch therefore, for ye know neither the day nor the hour wherein the Son of Man cometh.”

Mat. 25:13

Mat. 24:36

INQ.: It is true that, at first, the Apostles did not know the exact date of the Second Coming of the Saviour; however, from the time they were strengthened from on high at the descent of the Holy Spirit, they were made aware of all. For, as the Saviour foretold, by the Holy Spirit all the mysteries were revealed: “I have yet many things to say unto you, but ye cannot bear them now. Howbeit when he, the Spirit of truth, is come, he will guide you into all truth: for He shall not speak of Himself; but whatsoever He shall hear, that shall He speak: and He will shew you things to come.” From the time of the descent of the Holy Spirit at Pentecost, the Apostles—as well as all faithful Christians—with the illumination and wisdom given them by the Holy Spirit, were made able to know “all truth.” In other words, they became aware of the entirety of the divine plan for the history of the world and its end, and thus were able to determine, through Holy Scripture, the events of the future, such as the date of the Second Coming. Is not such a determination possible?

Jn. 16:12-13

EC: William Miller calculated that, according to Scripture, between the first of March 1843 and the first of March 1844, the Second Coming of Christ would take place. He had announced this date from as early as 1833 in the brochure "Prophecy from Holy Scripture of the Second Coming of the Lord in the year 1843." Another prophet, Joseph Chimes, had proposed—in the journals "The Voice of Midnight" (1842) and "The Bell of Danger"—that the Lord would come in the year 1843.

The closest disciple of Miller, a Mr. Snow, decided to add to the "prophecy" of Miller another seven months and ten days, predicting the date of the Second Coming of the Lord as the tenth of October 1844. He was also put to ridicule along with his teacher. Those who believed their pronouncements spent their fortunes, handing out all they had and buying white garments and candles in order to go out and meet the Lord. It is possible that the shop windows were even filled then with white garments for those travelling to heaven on the tenth of October 1844. Yet, this day passed like all others. The so-called "prophets" became the recipients of every kind of shame, derision, and mockery from those deluded people who had scattered their fortunes trusting in the false prophecies.

From these pitiful experiences, we must at least come to understand that the promise of our Saviour Jesus Christ concerning the revelation of the future by the Holy Spirit did not refer to the date of the Second Coming, as it appeared to many, but rather to prophecies pertaining to various events and signs due to come to pass in the Church. For, indeed, there have been revelations through the Holy Spirit, as we see, for example, in the Book of Revelation and other books of Holy Scripture. These revelations contain a variety of eschatological teachings (on the appearance of the Antichrist, of the false prophets, the unleashing of the persecutions of Christians). These revelations also contain the Apostles indis-

Mat. 10:19-20

pensable wisdom, which enabled them to present the divine teachings when they were led to give a defence before their accusers. These are the future events of which the Saviour speaks in the text that you read.

INQ.: The Apostle Paul writes: "But ye, brethren, are not in darkness, that that day should overtake you as a thief. Ye are all the children of light, and the children of the day: we are not of the night, nor of darkness." From these words, it follows that Christians can and should know the exact date of the Second Coming in order to be ready to accept it.

1 Thess. 5:4-5

EC: Why have you read from only verses four and five of chapter five from First Thessalonians, leaving out verses one and two, which serve to interpret verses four and five? Listen to what the Apostle Paul says there: "But of the times and the seasons, brethren, ye have no need that I write unto you. For yourselves know perfectly that the day of the Lord so cometh as a thief in the night." This is the truth to which Christ's Church has remained faithful. The true Church teaches, equally with the Apostle Paul, that the day of the Lord will come as a thief in the night and that no one knows the day nor the hour in which the Son of Man will come.

1 Thess. 5:1-2

It is possible only for the *approach* of the Second Coming to be known by the signs which must come before:

Mat. 24:24

- The preaching of the Gospel throughout the world.
- The turn of the Jews to Christianity after the preaching of the Gospel in the entire world.

Rom. 11:25-34

- The appearance of the Antichrist, also called the Man of Iniquity or the Beast, together with his representatives, pseudo-Christs, false prophets, and every type of false wonder worked by the power of Satan in order to

1 Jn. 2:18
2 Thess. 2:3-11
Rev. 13:1-8

Rev. 20:1-10

Mat. 24:9

Mat. 24:10-12

Mat. 24:6-7

Mat. 24:7-9

deceive the people. The Antichrist will sit in the place of God acting as if he were God, and—as an unrelenting beast—he will pursue with all rage and fury the chosen servants of God.

- The multiplication of wickedness and the growing cold of love between men, hatred and betrayal of one another.

- A torrent of bloodshed, wars and rumours of wars between nations, people and states.

- The appearance of calamities such as mass starvation, sicknesses, etc.

- The appearance of certain signs in the world such as the darkening of the sun and moon, the falling of stars from the sky, and the passing away of heaven and earth.

- The appearance in the heavens of the sign of the Son of Man, the True Cross, because this is the sign of victory of our Lord and no other sign so alerts us of His imminent arrival as does His Cross.

Mat. 24:32-33

The Lord explains these signs thus: "Now learn a parable of the fig tree; When his branch is yet tender, and putteth forth leaves, ye know that summer is nigh: So likewise ye, when ye shall see all these things, know that it is near, even at the doors." Therefore, concerning the signs that will precede the Second Coming of the Lord, we have explanations and confirmation from the Saviour Himself, while of the exact date of His coming, neither the angels nor even the Son of Man Himself, as man, are informed, but the Father alone knows.

The Holy Revelation of Saint John

Icon of the First Vision of the Apocalypse, located in the Cave
on the island of Patmos in which St. John beheld the Revelation.

CHAPTER 16

On the Thousand-Year Reign (Chiliasm)

INQUIRER: There are those who maintain that between the Second Coming of the Lord and the end of the world, Christ will reign upon the earth, governing—Himself along with His elect—for a thousand years. What is the truth of the matter, Father?

ELDER CLEOPA: This idea is an ancient one. In the first centuries of Christianity, it was endorsed by the so-called Chiliasts or Millenialists. Against them rose the entire ancient Church and its most important representatives.

The divine Fathers of the Church indicated in their writings that the one-thousand-year reign referred to in the book of Revelation signifies an infinite number of years, i.e. a kingdom that shall have no end. This we know well, since from Holy Scripture it is clear that the Kingdom of Christ is not of this world. In Holy Scripture, it is clearly indicated that the Kingdom of Heaven is also the Kingdom of God or Kingdom of Christ, insomuch as both Saint John the Forerunner and Christ Himself called it so. This Kingdom of Christ will be spiritual and will reign over the internal world of man, while externally being revealed

Jn. 18:36

Rom. 14:17   in the righteousness, peace, and joy of the Holy Spirit. Christ Himself established this kingdom and explained in His parables how it will appear, who it will include, and what power it will possess. His reign will not endure for only a thousand years, but
Lk. 1:33   eternally. Its inhabitants will include all faithful Christians from all the peoples of the world. It will reign over all creation, and it
Ps. 116: 1-2   will be a kingdom of righteousness. It will be a kingdom made
Dan. 7: 13-14
Mat. 28:18   up of souls—souls that have already entered and lived within it in this present life.

   This kingdom of Christ, derived not from this world, constitutes the Church, or the Body, of Christ, of which the
Eph. 1:22   head is Christ Himself. The adoption and entrance into this kingdom takes place only through the laver of regeneration or birth from above. No one can enter into this reign of God
Tit. 3:5
Jn. 3:3   except through baptism, which is to say, by being born again
Rom. 6:3   from above or being born of water and the spirit, according to the word of the Saviour: "Verily, verily, I say unto thee, Except a man be born of water and of the Spirit, he cannot
Jn. 3:5   enter into the kingdom of God." This heavenly birth by the power of the All-holy Spirit is a true resurrection from the dead, and hence the reason why Baptism is so often referred
Col. 2:12-13   to as "resurrection." Thus, also, it is that the Orthodox Chris-
Rom. 6:3-5   tian baptism is a renaissance of life and a resurrection from the dead. When the Apostle Paul writes, "Awake thou that sleepest, and arise from the dead, and Christ shall give thee
Eph. 5:14   light," he has in mind precisely this internal regeneration and resurrection through Christian Baptism, for no one can enter the Kingdom of Christ unless he has first been brought out from among the dead by Christian Baptism.

   Holy Scripture speaks to us about the thousand-year reign in prophetic and symbolic terms, corresponding to that which we spoke of above. Here is what Saint John the Evangelist says in his Revelation:

"And I saw an angel come down from heaven, having the key of the bottomless pit and a great chain in his hand. And he laid hold on the dragon, that old serpent, which is the Devil, and Satan, and bound him a thousand years, And cast him into the bottomless pit, and shut him up, and set a seal upon him, that he should deceive the nations no more, till the thousand years should be fulfilled: and after that he must be loosed a little season. And I saw thrones, and they sat upon them, and judgement was given unto them: and I saw the souls of them that were beheaded for the witness of Jesus, and for the word of God, and which had not worshipped the Beast, neither his image, neither had received his mark upon their foreheads, or in their hands; and they lived and reigned with Christ a thousand years. But the rest of the dead lived not again until the thousand years were finished. This is the first resurrection. Blessed and holy is he that hath part in the first resurrection: on such the second death hath no power, but they shall be priests of God and of Christ, and shall reign with him a thousand years. And when the thousand years are expired, Satan shall be loosed out of his prison, and shall go out to deceive the nations which are in the four quarters of the earth, Gog, and Magog, to gather them together to battle: the number of whom is as the sand of the sea. And they went up on the breadth of the earth, and compassed the camp of the saints about, and the beloved city: and fire came down from God out of heaven, and devoured them. And the Devil that deceived them was cast into the lake of fire and brimstone, where the Beast and the False Prophet are, and shall be tormented day and night forever and ever. And I saw a great white throne, and him that sat on it, from whose face the earth and the heaven fled away; and there was found no place for them. And I saw the dead, small and great, stand before God; and the books were opened: and another book was opened, which is the book of life: and the dead were judged out of those things which were written in the books, according to their works. And the sea gave up the dead which were in it; and death and hell delivered up the dead which were in them: and they were judged every man according to their works. And death and hell were cast into the lake of fire. This is the second death."

Rev. 20:1-14

From this passage we can ascertain the following:

verses 1-2

1) The thousand-year reign of Christ is a period in which Christ has bound the power of the Devil over men.

verse 3

2) At the end of this period, the Devil will again be lord over men and oppress them, but only for a season.

verses 4-5

3) The members of this kingdom will be those alone who do not submit to the Beast and accept his engraved seal, and who have a part in the first resurrection.

verse 5

4) Those who were not worthy of this resurrection will be raised at the end of the thousand years, that is at the second resurrection, as this resurrection, relative to the first, is the second.

verse 6

5) Death will have no power over the sharers in the thousand-year reign.

6) At the end of these thousand years and after a gruesomely violent persecution against the saints, the Devil and his followers will be cast into the lake of fire—the second death.

verses 4-15

From this, it should be abundantly clear that the thousand-year kingdom is nothing else but the Kingdom of God or Kingdom of Heaven, and this is clear, seeing that:

1) In the period of this reign, the Devil was bound and loosed, receiving power over men. Christ entered into His dominion and bound the Devil; that is, by the redemption of humanity by His Blood, He bound and restrained his power over mankind.

2) The entrance into this kingdom presupposes the first resurrection, that is, none other than holy Baptism itself—often, in fact, called by the name of resurrection, or being born again from above, or simply regeneration. This resurrection through Baptism is "the first," in comparison to "the second," the general one, of the body, which is also called the last resurrection, as when Martha spoke to Christ concerning her brother: "I know that he shall rise again at the resurrection on the Last Day."

Jn. 11:24

3) At the end of this kingdom or reign, the Devil will again be let loose to deceive the people and with power and mania to assault and oppress holy Christians in the person of the Antichrist, the Beast or the False Prophet.

Rev. 13:1-11

Mat. 24:22
Rev. 13:5, 20:3

4) The duration of this period will be brief; and yet, it will constitute one of the signs signalling the immediacy of the Second Coming of Christ.

Therefore, it should be clearly known that the first resurrection is the baptismal resurrection, and the second resurrection is that which we await on "the last day," the last resurrection. Furthermore, it should also be clear that the first death is the natural one or the separation of the soul from the body, while the second death is the eternal torment [of hell], so called due to its opposition to the blessed life of eternity. It should also be clear that this second death has no power over those made worthy of the first resurrection. Likewise, from this it follows that the first death, from which not even the saints are delivered, is the natural or bodily death.

Mat. 18:8

Jn. 5:24

In Holy Scripture, someone's sinful condition is also compared to a kind of death. It is with this meaning that the Saviour says to one of His disciples who had asked leave to first go and bury his father, "Follow me, and let the dead bury their dead." Likewise does He speak with this in mind when saying, "He that believeth in Me, though he were dead, yet shall he live; and whosoever liveth and believeth in me shall never die." The Apostle also had this meaning in mind when he wrote, "reckon ye also yourselves to be dead indeed unto sin, but alive unto God through Jesus Christ our Lord." Moreover, with this meaning as well, is it written to the angel (ἐπίσκοπο) of the Church in Sardis: "I know thy works, and that thou hast a name that thou livest, but thou art dead." This does not, however, constitute the first death, as the baptismal resurrection constitutes the first resurrection: considering that this death is a condition that *leads to* but is not already the fact of death. When we spoke of "resurrection" and "death" above, we had in mind not merely a condition or state but a specific action or event—of resurrection and of death, respectively.

Mat. 8:22

Jn. 11:25

Rom. 6:11, 8:10

Rev. 3:1

Although the duration of the reign of Christ is designated, on the whole, as a thousand years, we should understand this to signify an era immeasurable and undesignated. Therefore, its length is nothing else except the period between the first and second comings of the Lord or, more precisely, the period of the consolidation of the Kingdom of God until His Second Coming. This is the explanation of the Kingdom of God and its duration upon this earth.

INQ.: Father, recently I had a very disturbing conversation with some people concerning this question and came away with the opinion that the thousand-year reign could only be understood in earthly terms. This must be the case seeing that it will be inaugurated at the Second Coming, preceded by the resurrection of the righteous who in turn will reign with Christ for a thousand years, after which will occur the resurrection of sinners, the judgement, and the end of the world.

verses 4-5

This interpretation seems to me to proceed from the twentieth chapter of Revelation that you read earlier. It can be deduced from that chapter that there will be "final resurrections:" the first resurrection of the righteous at the beginning of the thousand years and the second resurrection of the sinful at the end of the world.

During the period of a thousand years, the active power of the Devil will be restricted up until just before the end when, after a brief but horrible flurry of aggression, he will be thrown into Hades together with all of his servants. Afterward, they will be resurrected, judged and condemned to eternal punishment. After the first period, we will pass through to the end of the world. This is, for example, what the Apostle Paul says when writing to the Christians of Thessalonica: "For if we believe that Jesus died and rose again, even so them also which sleep in Jesus will God bring with him. For this we say unto you by the word of the Lord,

verses 7-14

verses 12-15

verse 11

that we which are alive and remain unto the coming of the Lord shall not prevent them which are asleep. For the Lord Himself shall descend from heaven with a shout, with the voice of the archangel, and with the trump of God: and the dead in Christ shall rise first." Consequently, at His Second Coming, Christ will raise those who have died faithful to Him (i.e. those which, as the Apostle says, "shall rise first"); hence, [this is] the first resurrection. The resurrection of the dead, or the second resurrection, will follow later—He does not tell us exactly when—but according to Revelation it will be after a thousand years. Listen to what Saint Paul says about this: "But every man in his own order: Christ the first fruits; afterward they that are Christ's at His coming." In other words, the Just join the choir of the Righteous at the beginning of the thousand-year reign and the sinful join an assembly of their own at the end of the thousand-year period. Is this not the truth of the matter, Father?

1 Thess. 4:14-16

1 Cor. 15:23

EC: As I explained to you earlier, the True Church of Christ understands the "millennium" of Holy Scripture mystically and symbolically to mean an indeterminate number of years. Do you think that Scripture only in this passage speaks in a mystical and veiled manner, or could it be that many hard to comprehend subjects are approached in this way? Are there not, in fact, many mystical, symbolic, and allegorical expressions or events that cannot be explained literally but carry exalted and spiritual meanings often completely different from that readily apparent? How can we explain the book of Revelation literally when it is bound with seven seals? What is the red horse that is like unto fire? And what of the seven angels who were given seven plagues? How should we understand them?

Rev. 5:1

Rev. 6:4

Rev. 15:1-7

There are those who speak of two resurrections at the end of the world, and thus, according to them, somehow a third coming of the Lord must take place. However, such a thing is surely not true. It was shown above that the first resurrection is realized through Christian baptism and the second is the last (εσχάτη) or general resurrection [of the body]. Saint John the Evangelist renders precisely the words of the Saviour concerning the two resurrections: "Verily, verily, I say unto you, He that heareth my word, and believeth on him that sent me, hath everlasting life, and shall not come into condemnation; but is passed from death unto life. Verily, verily, I say unto you, The hour is coming, and now is, when the dead shall hear the voice of the Son of God: and they that hear shall live." As this passage concerns the resurrection of those who will hear the voice of the Son of God, i.e. the resurrection which "now is": this cannot be interpreted as referring to the last resurrection but only to the present resurrection of those who are raised from the death of sin to the life of Christ: to the new life of Christian faith entered–as the Apostle and Evangelist himself relates elsewhere–through Christian Baptism. This is the first resurrection referred to in the book of Revelation.

Jn. 5:24-25

Jn. 5:24-25

Further on, the Saviour speaks about another kind of resurrection—a resurrection which even now is, and yet will, however, happen at the end of the world—which is not of the soul but of the body and, specifically, of the dead in the graves: "Marvel not at this: for the hour is coming, in which all that are in the graves shall hear his voice, and shall come forth; they that have done good, unto the resurrection of life; and they that have done evil, unto the resurrection of damnation." In other words, marvel not at the power of Christ to raise spiritually (i.e. in the first resurrection), for, indeed, He will raise all the dead from the graves as well. This passage

Jn. 5:28-29

excludes outright the possibility of there being a period of a thousand years between the resurrection of the righteous and the resurrection of the sinful, for it clearly shows that the last or general resurrection is one and only and will happen to all. This is the second resurrection. As for the first, we saw that it is that resurrection which "now is," the present resurrection, and not the general or last resurrection.

Thus, through an analysis and comparison of the passages of Holy Scripture, we see how their meaning is clarified and elucidated, and how the possibility of an interpolation of a one-thousand-year period between the two resurrections is ruled out. According to the teaching of the true Church of Christ, the one-thousand-year period should be understood as extending between the first resurrection, which happens in Christian Baptism, and the second or last resurrection.

1 Thess. 4:14-16 This is, in fact, what we find in Saint Paul's first letter to the Thessalonians, where he speaks only of one resurrection and not a second or last resurrection. It is true that here Saint Paul is referring to the resurrection of the Just who have fallen asleep in the Lord and not to the resurrection of sinners. However, this is not because they will be raised later, after a thousand years, but simply because the Apostle Paul and his listeners are only concerned about the fate of those "asleep in Christ." The fact that he makes no reference to sinners does not mean that they will be raised a thousand years later. The Apostle is not in the least concerned here with other questions, for his aim in this epistle is to comfort his

verse 18 readers, that they be not sorrowful, anxious, or in ignorance concerning the fate of those reposed in Christ.

1 Cor. 15:23 In his first epistle to the Corinthians, Saint Paul speaks of there being "orders." The Chiliasts wrongly interpret this passage as referring only to two orders—namely, of the Just and of the Sinful, whose resurrections will be separated by a

see
verses 39-41
period of one thousand years. In truth, Saint Paul is speaking here of many orders, analogous to the degree of holiness or sinfulness ("for one differeth from another in glory") with which they will be revealed.

Holy Scripture is explicit and categorical in many places concerning the Second Coming of Christ, specifically, that it will be one single date for all, righteous and sinners alike, without there being a period of one thousand years between the resurrection and judgement of some and that of others. The Saviour said: "For the hour is coming, in which all that are in the graves shall hear his voice, and shall come forth; they that have done good, unto the resurrection of life; and they that have done evil, unto the resurrection of damnation." Hence, there will be one voice alone announcing the resurrection of all. In another place the Lord also says:

Jn. 5:28-29

> "When the Son of man shall come in his glory, and all the holy angels with him, then shall he sit upon the throne of his glory: And before him shall be gathered all nations: and he shall separate them one from another, as a shepherd divideth his sheep from the goats: And he shall set the sheep on his right hand, but the goats on the left. Then shall the King say unto them on his right hand, Come, ye blessed of my Father, inherit the kingdom prepared for you from the foundation of the world . . . Then shall he say also unto them on the left hand, Depart from me, ye cursed, into everlasting fire . . ."

Mat. 25:31-46

Here, the Saviour speaks with precision and clarity concerning His Second Coming and future judgement. In this most glorious parable, He communicates the following certainty: there will be one harvest for the wheat and the tares alike; the Bridegroom will come for all the virgins at one

Mat. 13:30, 42-3

Mat. 25:1-13

Mat. 25:14-30

and the same time; and, in the same hour, a reckoning will be sought for the work done by the servants entrusted with the talents. Therefore, once is the last advent of Christ, once is the resurrection and appearance of all before the King and Judge, and once is the judgement of mankind.

INQ.: I read in a brochure that the date of the beginning of the millennium can be determined, and that it will not be identical with the date of the Second Coming, and that it represents the end of the "era of idol-worship." Does this have any validity?

EC: First of all, know with absolute assurance that there does not exist any such millennium with the meaning conveyed in that brochure. If the date of the Second Coming of Christ cannot be determined, as neither the Angels nor even the Son of Man, as man, have been informed of it, then surely neither can the date of the beginning of the "millennium" be determined.

Mat. 24:36-44

We know that in that which pertains to salvation, the history of the world can only be divided into two periods: that of the Old Testament and that of the New Testament. Another age will begin with the Second Coming of our Lord, but this will be the last and everlasting age. In the history of the world, there existed other lesser episodes, which subdivided the two great periods without thereby constituting two or three more periods. Ages or epochs that we have with this meaning include those of the Patriarchs, the Apostles, the persecutions, and so on.

Concerning the passages of the Old Testament, these cannot be understood as if they were magical, but are either factual or symbolic, like the book from which they are derived. How can someone know that the six days of creation were, in actuality, some seven thousand years and that they each represent a great duration of time for humanity or even one thousand years?

Nowhere does it say in Holy Scripture that one day is equal to one thousand years, but only that before the creation of the visible world, time did not exist. Time, for God, is not fixed or appointed, but, rather, one day before God is considered as a thousand years and a thousand years as one day or as a night watch. It does not follow from this that figures from Holy Scripture represent a certain number of days, which we then reckon as years. In this way precisely would we then also be able to consider that which they represent as a thousand years. Conversely, we would also be able to say, with the same logic, that the thousand years of the millennium really means one day. And in this case, what would remain any longer of the calculations and analysis of the Millennialists? All their calculations are contradictory and refuted by the truth of things.

INQ.: With respect to that which is said in the Symbol of Faith, the Nicene-Constantinopolitan Creed, "And His kingdom shall have no end," the Chiliasts say that the Lord will come before the Future Judgement to rule with them a thousand years, and that, afterward, he will raise the sinners to be judged. Is it not true that the Lord will rule endlessly after the final judgement?

EC: The True Church tells us that the kingdom of the Lord will have no end. The Reign of Jesus Christ, as man, and His Glory will never come to an end, but will endure eternally. For, on the one hand, Jesus is not only human, from whom God could someday take His glory. On the other hand, as the Son of God, He will never deny His human nature. His

Margin notes:
2 Pet. 3:8

325 & 381 AD

being a man, so filled with divine glory, will never come to an end.

The everlasting Reign of Jesus Christ was announced in advance by the Archangel Gabriel. It is true, as Saint Paul says, that Christ will be subjected in everything to the Father and that, afterward, He will subject everything to Himself. Yet, this means the submission of the entire world before the Father and the cessation of His redemptive activity, as it is His own work, which He assumed at His incarnation.

So, let the Chiliasts know that they cannot make human calculations and determinations for mysteries that are unknown to the angels, and even, in His humanity, to the Son of God Himself.

CHAPTER 17

On the Eternal Torments of Hell

INQUIRER: I have heard that some Christians say that it is impossible for hell to be eternal since this would come into conflict with the goodness of God.

ELDER CLEOPA: We know well from solid testimonies of Holy Scripture that for evildoers the torments of hell will be eternal. Listen to what the holy Evangelist says concerning this: "Then shall He say also unto them on the left hand, depart from me, ye cursed, into everlasting fire, prepared for the devil and his angels." Further on, when showing the result of the future judgement, he says, "And these shall go away into everlasting punishment: but the righteous into life eternal." Likewise, the Saviour, desiring to define the permanence of the torments of hell, called them "hell fire, where their worm dieth not, and the fire is not quenched." In another passage, the Saviour, referring again to the enduring nature of the torments of hell, says: "Wherefore if thy hand or thy foot offend thee, cut them off, and cast them from thee: it is better for thee to enter into life halt or maimed, rather than having two hands or two feet to be cast into everlasting

Mat. 25:41

Mat. 25:46

Mk. 9:43-48

Mat. 18:8 fire." The Prophet Isaiah certifying the truth of the eternal fire of hell, says the following: "And they shall go forth, and look upon the carcasses of the men that have transgressed against me: for their worm shall not die, neither shall their fire be quenched; and they shall be an abhorring unto all Is. 66:24 flesh." Whereas the Prophet Daniel, describes the same when saying: "And many of them that sleep in the dust of the earth shall awake, some to everlasting life, and some to shame and Dan. 12:2 everlasting contempt." The word "many" here means all, for Daniel when speaking about "the many" means the mass of reposed that will be raised.

INQ.: There are those who maintain that the torments of hell cannot be eternal since we read in Holy Scripture: "The last 1 Cor. 15:26 enemy that shall be destroyed is death." From this it follows that death, or in other words hell, will not exist. Consequently, that which is called hell or eternal death will not exist except as a destruction or annihilation of evildoers in Rev. 20:9 order that they not remain unto eternity. Hell is, according to my opinion, nothing other than the Jewish Sheol, which signifies the pit of the grave in the soil. Furthermore, the words "fire" and "torment" do not mean something eternal, but only death, the placement into the ground. For man does not have an immortal soul and that is why death means return of man into the earth.

EC: If it is as you say, then neither should the future judgement exist, for it will have been stripped of all meaning. We know, however, from both the Holy Scriptures and the Holy Fathers and universal teachers of our Church that the final or future judgement will happen. This can be said to be so for these four reasons: 1) to reveal the righteousness of God, 2) to reveal the injustices of men, 3) to reward the good works of the righteous, and 4) to chastise the unrepentant evildoers with the eternal torments.

If man is only dust and earth, without a soul, how is it that some have, in spite of that, been resurrected? How is it possible, moreover, that the Saviour teaches us to honour and value the soul more than the body, and further, to seek not deeds for the body but for the soul: deeds that, like the soul, are imperishable? In our discussion about the honour due the saints, I gave you many examples of this. Our Saviour teaches us that our soul is more valuable than all the world and that it is immortal. Our Saviour tells us that hell is the place of eternal suffering. The divine Scriptures show us that in hell, the body as well as the soul suffers from the eternal torments and that the punishment is eternal.

INQ.: There is also another very old view that God is All-Good, that His love is unlimited toward man, and because of this, it is practically impossible for Him to chastise men with eternal suffering. He is the Father of all, and what kind of Father would chastise His disobedient children with eternal torture? Is not a father always disposed to forgive his children? Would not our heavenly Father be so much more disposed to mercy and forbearance toward us?

EC: Truly, God is forgiving and long-suffering towards those who fall into sin in this life, for the time of our correction is now, in this life, and the acquisition of His forgiveness depends on our own repentance. In the life on the other side of the grave, however, we are no longer able to repent—to change our minds—given that, there, God does not judge us according to His omnipotence and goodness but in accord with His impartiality and righteousness, rewarding each

Margin references:
Mat. 16:26
Mk. 8:36
Mat. 22:31
Mat. 18:8
Dt. 21:21
Mk. 9:43
Mat. 5:22
Mk. 3:29

Jn. 9:4

Mat. 10:41
Mat. 25:35

according to his deeds. If God were to forgive all the sins of men without justice or fairness, what would be the point of continually alarming us with the terror of the eternal torments if, in fact, they did not exist? How is it possible for God to tell us lies instead of the truth?

INQ.: Nevertheless, how is it that for a few sins committed in this passing life, someone will earn torments for eternity? Chastisement must be commensurate with the unresponsiveness of the sinner and with reference to the seriousness of the sin. A short-lived sin cannot be punished with an eternal punishment, for this would mean an unjust judgement on the part of God, who is called Just and All-Good.

EC: In this case, neither should the blessedness of the righteous be eternal, for the same analogy and relationship exists between this joy and the worthiness of the deeds. Is it possible for the reward and the blessedness of the just to abide eternally, while the suffering and the chastisement of those who are worthy of hell is temporary? God offers eternal joy to the righteous, who struggled for a time to carry out good works here on earth. But, as a just and righteous God, He also eternally chastises the ungodly that transgressed in this temporal life. Why is it so? Because the wounds incurred from sin that are not healed in this life through the appropriate repentance will remain infected eternally in the presence of God. If we mock and scorn the Person of God by committing sins with our free will, we must nevertheless remember that His glory, power and righteousness, and all His divine characteristics have no end. In the same way, on account of the sins we have not repented for, the torments of hell will also be unending.[1]

Have you not heard of or seen in this present life the many cases when someone, due to the sins he has committed at one time or another, received a punishment which lasted many years or even until the end of his life? The duration of time in which the evil act was committed is not what is condemnatory and determinative of the imposition of the punishment, but its gravity and extent. The man who, with an automatic machine gun, cuts down one hundred people in one minute, even though he committed such mass murder in such a short period of time, will not be punished for his crime for only one minute. It must be clear that he who dies in grave and disastrous sins is separated from God forever and, in particular, he will not be able, in the next life, to be amended. In the life beyond the grave, his sins will remain with him eternally and thus the torments will also continue to exist forever.

Jn. 9:4

INQ.: Are the other testimonies in Holy Scripture supportive of the endlessness of the torments of hell?

EC: There are many. If you are interested, read the following passages of Holy Scripture: Mat. 18:8, 23:33, and 25:41-46, Mk. 3:29 and 9:44, Lk. 3:17, 1 Thess. 1:9, Heb. 10:27, Rev. 14:11 and 20:10, Isa. 33:14 and 66:24, and Dan. 12:2, and elsewhere.

Nihilism, by Fr. Seraphim Rose, Fr. Seraphim Rose Foundation, p. 99

1 Hell is the love of God rejected: "For most men today "life" is a small thing, a fleeting thing of small affirmation and small denial, veiled in comforting illusions and the hopeful prospect of ultimate nothingness. . . . But God loves even such men too much to allow them simply to "forget" Him and "pass away" . . . out of His presence which alone is life to men; He offers, even to those in Hell, His Love, which is torment to those who have not prepared themselves in this life to receive it."

Icon from the Holy Monastery of Stavronikita, Mount Athos (16th century).

The Descent of the Holy Spirit at Pentecost

"And there appeared unto them cloven tongues like as of fire, and it sat upon each of them. And they were all filled with the Holy Ghost, and began to speak with other tongues, as the Spirit gave them utterance."

CHAPTER 18

On Speaking in Tongues[1]

INQUIRER: What is *glossolalia* or "speaking in tongues"?

ELDER CLEOPA: *Glossolalia*, or "speaking in tongues," as a gift of the Holy Spirit, is the ability to speak a foreign language without having to be taught it or knowing it beforehand.[2] This is clear from the Holy Scriptures, in which the events of Pentecost are described, and at which time this divine gift first appeared. The text is unabbreviated and unambiguous and recounts for us an actual event. Consequently, the text itself cannot be explained with some particular mystical or spiritual meaning alone, omitting the literal meaning.

Let's allow the passage itself, from the Acts of the Apostles, to explain what the text means and what comprises

1 Due to confusion caused by earlier translations into English, γλωσσολαλία has been rendered here variously as "*glossolalia,*" "speaking a foreign language," "speaking a foreign tongue," and "speaking in tongues."

2 Fr. Cleopa, following St. John Chrysostom, sees in the gift of tongues only that of speaking a foreign language. For an interpretation in which the gift of tongues is understood to also mean the Jesus Prayer or Prayer of the Heart, see *Church, Synods and Civilizations* by Fr. John Romanides, as well as the study by Hieromonk Alexis of Karakalou, *In Peace Let us Pray to the Lord.*

the speaking of foreign tongues by the Grace of the Holy Spirit:

"And when the day of Pentecost was fully come, they were all with one accord in one place. And suddenly there came a sound from heaven as of a rushing mighty wind, and it filled all the house where they were sitting. And there appeared unto them cloven tongues like as of fire, and it sat upon each of them. And they were all filled with the Holy Ghost, and began to speak with other tongues, as the Spirit gave them utterance. And there were dwelling at Jerusalem Jews, devout men, out of every nation under heaven. Now when this was noised abroad, the multitude came together, and were confounded, because that every man heard them speak in his own language. And they were all amazed and marvelled, saying one to another, Behold, are not all these which speak Galilaeans? And how hear we every man in our own tongue, wherein we were born? Parthians, and Medes, and Elamites, and the dwellers in Mesopotamia, and in Judaea, and Cappadocia, in Pontus, and Asia, Phrygia, and Pamphylia, in Egypt, and in the parts of Libya about Cyrene, and strangers of Rome, Jews and proselytes, Cretes and Arabians, we do hear them speak in our tongues the wonderful works of God. And they were all amazed, and were in doubt, saying one to another, What meaneth this? Others mocking said, These men are full of new wine."

Acts 2:1-13

From an examination of these thirteen verses that contain the key to the solution of the problem, we can educe the following conclusions:

- The speaking of foreign tongues or languages, by the grace of the Holy Spirit, manifested itself, as a miracle, for the first time in history. For this reason, the reader is provided with an extensive description, that he may be able to learn what this miracle is and in what it consists.

- With this powerful gift of the Holy Spirit, the Apostles began to preach in other languages, even 15 different local languages of other tribes and nations that had converged there for the Feast of Pentecost.

- The Jews of other nations, who had as their mother tongue the language of the nation in which they lived, marvelled when they heard the Apostles preach in their own language, for the Apostles were simple men of Galilee and it was impossible for them to know another language except the Aramaic they had learned at home.

- The Jews of other nations understood everything from the divine preaching of the Apostles. They spoke to them with precision in their own language concerning the greatness of God without needing a translator, and it is in exactly this that the miracle rests. The visitors to Jerusalem were unable to explain what they witnessed and were full of wonder.

- Among the listeners of the preaching, there were also some that did not understand anything that the Apostles said and subsequently mocked the Apostles, thinking that they were drunk. This group can be none other than the residents of Jerusalem, and perhaps those of nearby Palestine, who did not know other languages except their mother tongue, Aramaic. For these men, the preaching of the Apostles was completely unintelligible and they considered it simply gibberish.

Thus, the residents did not understand anything from the preaching unless someone translated it for them. For just as there is the gift of speaking in tongues or foreign languages, there also exists the gift of translation. This was given, as is apparent below, when those listening were only locals ignorant of other languages, as was, for example, the case in Corinth. In Jerusalem, however, during this period, there was not felt this deficiency. The gift of translation was itself also miraculous, just as was that of *glossolalia*, on which it was directly dependent. Not having this gift, the residents who were listening judged the work of the Apostles according to their personal judgement and perception alone.

Glossolalia was a sign of the power of God and, as a decisive means of evangelism, was manifested among men who ignored the Faith. For, apart from this, what meaning does it have for someone to speak about Christ in a foreign language if he was taught, believed, and lived his faith in Christ from his childhood years?

If there are those who speak foreign languages and they are not understood by anyone, how do they build up the Church or benefit it? For the purpose of *glossolalia* was for the Apostles to be able to spread, through the transmission of the *kerygma* (preaching) in foreign languages, the Faith of Christians to all people and to make the Gospel known throughout the world, as it is written: "Their sound hath gone forth into all the earth, and their words unto the ends of the world."

If someone had this gift, we must not think that it was the greatest among the gifts of God. The Apostle Paul says that there are other, greater gifts of the Holy Spirit than that of *glossolalia*. "I would that ye all spake with tongues but rather that ye prophesied: for greater is he that prophesieth than he that speaketh with tongues, except he interpret, that the

1 Cor. 14

1 Cor. 14:21-25

Ps. 18:4

1 Cor. 14:5

church may receive edification." And elsewhere he also says, "If therefore the whole church be come together into one place, and all speak with tongues, and there come in those that are unlearned, or unbelievers, will they not say that ye

1 Cor. 14:23

are mad?"

Consequently, the gifts of prophecy, of preaching, and of interpretation of Scripture are much higher than the gift of *glossolalia* because, with these, the Church of Christ is built up and benefitted much more than with the gift of linguistics

1 Cor. 14:2-4

or speaking different languages. More sublime and higher than all the gifts is love, about which [you should] listen to what the Apostle Paul has to say: "Though I speak with the tongues of men and of angels, and have not charity, I am

1 Cor. 13:1

become as sounding brass, or a tinkling cymbal."

INQ.: It is claimed by certain people that when the grace of the Holy Spirit comes to them and they begin to speak in tongues, they find themselves in a state of ecstasy. It is only at this time that they are able to speak certain inarticulate and incomprehensible human sounds, to have certain internal impulses or exclamations of joy, or to voice a certain remorse for their sins, as well as other movements of the body which are made by the action of the grace of the Holy Spirit. Saul had a similar spiritual manifestation when following David and going to Ramah. He was overcome by the prophetic spirit and, with a flurry, he prophesied, ripped his clothes

1 Sam. 19:22-24

off, and went naked all day and all night.

EC: It is incomprehensible for a healthy, clear, and well-balanced intellect to reveal the great mysteries of God with inarticulate exclamations. Such a thing is not at all the same, as we know from that which was revealed through *glossolalia*

1 Cor. 14:2-4

as a divine gift.

The Greek idol-worshipers of antiquity had similar exhibitions when they prayed to their gods Dionysus, Zeus, and the others. When they were found before a diabolic idol, they would fall into ecstasy or a trance, shaking and making rhythmic movements with their body, and tumble on the ground, with a few even foaming at the mouth like the demon-possessed of olden times. Next, they would get up and sing rhapsodic melodies and make exclamations with demonic delight. The same happened with the Montanists, heretics of the first and second centuries after Christ, the Gnostics—and, later, the Methodists, the Quakers, the Pentecostals, and others. These groups took to making uncanny and strange turns and movements of the body, had hallucinations and were in delusion, and thought that all of this came from God when, in actuality, it comes from theologians of darkness who are familiar with Holy Scripture and who lead into delusion the unsuspecting, cheating them with words taken even from Holy Scripture.

INQ.: These people also say that, with the charisma of speaking in tongues that they possess, they maintain unbroken the work of the Holy Spirit among men and within the Church of Christ as it existed in the beginning of Christianity. For—they claim—today, as also in the beginning, with this perceptible sign of the gift of grace, the Holy Spirit stirs wonder and amazement in those who are not yet Christians. Furthermore, with this visible sign of the gift of speaking in tongues, it becomes known to the faithful that there still exists a work of the Holy Spirit in the Church, as in the first period of Christians in Jerusalem.

EC: The gift of speaking in foreign tongues or *glossolalia* was not given by God for all time, until the end of the world. It was a sign given to the Church only for a time, with the aim of making it easier for those of other religions to convert to Christianity. We see, in this respect, that the Jews of Jerusalem, who did not understand the preaching of the Apostles—*kerygma* given by Divine Grace—did not, in fact, believe, but rather said that the Apostles were drunk. The Prophet Isaiah prophesied concerning their disbelief before this great gift of grace, saying, "For with stammering lips and another tongue will he speak to this people. To whom he said, This is the rest wherewith ye may cause the weary to rest; and this is the refreshing: yet they would not hear." Indeed, in Jerusalem they spoke to them with lips of strangers, for the foreign Jews, or Jews of the Diaspora, heard about the wondrous works of God in their own languages and believed; and thus, the Apostle Paul prophesied that the gift of speaking in foreign tongues would cease.

Is. 28:11-12

Acts 2:11
1 Cor. 13:8
1 Cor. 14:22-28

The people of that time were spiritually in the age of infancy—for only just recently had they left the worship of idols—and their intellects were blurred, confused, and insensible. They were still captives to the enjoyment of the fleshly pleasures and did not have knowledge of the divine gifts that one enjoys only on account of faith. It is for this reason that signs and wonders were then showered upon them.

Some spiritual gifts are invisible and become accessible to man through faith. Others, however, are visible on account of the unbelief of men. Here is an example: The forgiveness of sins is an invisible spiritual work. We do not see with our sensible eyes how we are purified of our sins. Why? Because neither is the soul that is purified visible to the eyes of our body. Speaking in different tongues or languages is also a work of the Holy Spirit, but it is a visible sign and more easily persuades those of other religions; hence, this is the reason Saint Paul says the following:

"Wherefore tongues are for a sign, not to them that believe, but to them that believe not: but prophesying serveth not for them that believe not, but for them which believe." He who believes does not have need of guarantees and signs. The first Christians would not have believed if they had not received signs.

1 Cor. 14:22

INQ.: From those with whom I spoke I learned that besides the gift of speaking in tongues, they have also the gift of the baptism of "the Holy Spirit and fire," which is totally different from baptism with water. This baptism showers upon them various miraculous gifts of the Holy Spirit, especially that of glossolalia and the interpretation of Scripture, as happened also at Pentecost with the Apostles.

Lk. 3:16

EC: Is it possible that there are two Christian Baptisms? Does it not say in Holy Scripture that there is one and only one? St. Paul tells us there is but "one Lord, one faith, one baptism, one God and Father of all . . ." The baptism of "the Holy Spirit and fire" of Pentecost is none other than the Christian Baptism that was pre-announced by both Saint John the Baptist and the Saviour Himself and which He said would happen by "water and the Spirit"—a baptism neither by water alone, as with the baptism of John, nor only by the Spirit. These two elements, the one visible and the other invisible, constitute the two most necessary prerequisites for the one and only Christian Baptism. If, with respect to the practice of this mystery, some still speak only of water or only of the Spirit as constituting the main element of this Mystery, let them know that the Mystery is one and only one, and that its two elements are inseparable.

Eph. 4:5
[see also
1 Cor. 12:13]
Lk. 3:16
Mat. 3:11
Acts 1:5
Jn. 3:5

INQ.: Each Christian should have within him the Holy Spirit. The members of a certain Christian brotherhood say that while they can give evidence of the presence of the Holy Spirit within them through the practice of speaking in foreign speech, the Orthodox are not able to show this by any means. Consequently, they say that the Orthodox are not true Christians, due to the absence of this work of the Holy Spirit in their lives.

EC: It is true that each Christian should have consciously within himself the Holy Spirit. Yet, the presence of the Holy Spirit is not only made manifest through *glossolalia*. The Apostle Paul tells us that "the fruit of the Spirit is love, joy, peace, longsuffering, gentleness, goodness, faith, meekness, temperance . . ." Do you see, therefore, that among the fruits of the Holy Spirit, the practice of speaking in foreign languages is not referred to anywhere? This is because it is a gift of the Holy Spirit that was given for a certain period of time in the Church, whereas the gifts referred to here by the Apostle, all Christians of every epoch must have throughout their lives. Whoever has the fruits of the Spirit has also the Holy Spirit within him. The gift of *glossolalia* is not a common gift of grace but something special and not given to everyone. How, then, can we consider it a precondition of salvation and a prerequisite for the presence of the Holy Spirit in our life when it is not given to everyone? The Apostle Paul says, "Do all speak in tongues?" Consequently, then, those who do not speak in tongues can also be good Christians. In the community of true Christians, everyone does not have the same gifts. The Apostles did not require this gift from all the Christians, and indeed, in quite a few, it was revealed that this talent was profitless. The Apostles themselves did not use this gift, apart from exceptional cases when they had a certain aim, as on the day of Pentecost. So, therefore, it should be clear that they did not call upon every Christian to have this gift as a means of salvation.

Gal. 5:22-23

1 Cor. 12:10

1 Cor. 12:30

INQ.: I would like for you, after all that we have said concerning *glossolalia*, to summarize the main points of our discussion.

EC: Listen, brother, and guard well within your mind: true *glossolalia*, as a gift of the Holy Spirit, can be recognized only when it is combined with the following presuppositions.

1) If someone, by inspiration of the Holy Spirit, speaks a language, it should be understood by all those who stand nearby, just as it happened in the case that we cited from the Acts of the Apostles.

Acts 2:1-13

2) When someone speaks a language among the residents [of Jerusalem, Corinth, etc.] that they do not understand, then another gift, the gift of translation of this language into the language of the people is necessary. Without this translation, the foreign language is babbling and lunacy.

1 Cor. 14:23

3) Glossolalia was not given to the Church forever, but only in the beginning of Christianity, in order to awaken the idol-worshippers and Jews to belief in Christ. This is why the Apostle Paul said that the gift of *glossolalia* would, at some point, cease to exist in the Church.

1 Cor. 13:8

4) Since we believe that Christ is our true God, we no longer have need of *glossolalia*, given the fact that the knowledge of foreign languages by inspiration of the Holy Spirit is a sign (miracle) necessary only for the unbelieving and not for the faithful.

1 Cor. 14:22

5) From the beginning of Christianity, *glossolalia* was among the lesser gifts in the Church of Christ, while

the others—such as that of prophecy, of interpretation of Scripture, of love, and of the rest—were much greater.

6) It is totally out of the question for speaking in tongues, as a gift of the Holy Spirit, to mean a delirium in a non-existent and incomprehensible language, for then it would not be speaking in languages but in our own [exclusive] language. Moreover, it comes into clear contradiction with chapter two of the Acts of the Apostles.

Mk. 16:17

7) The inarticulate voices, lunacies, and incoherent utterances which we often hear from the self-proclaimed speakers of tongues very much resemble the scenes the idol-worshippers would make before their idols of Dionysius—as well as with quite a few of the Montanists, Gnostics, Quakers, and (later) Pentecostals, all of whom the true Church of Christ anathematizes.

See the first and second Canons of the Sixth Oecumenical Council

Thus, brother, foreign to the Spirit of God is the speaking in tongues of those who think they are grace-bearers and make bold to misrepresent the true *glossolalia*, a gift of the Holy Spirit that existed at the outset of Christianity.

CHAPTER 19

On Magic and Occultism

INQUIRER: I know that many people, in pain caused by the death of their beloved relatives, take recourse to spiritualism, fortune-telling, occultism, or even aim at conversing with their dead relatives. Why does the Church not allow this?

ELDER CLEOPA: In both Holy Scripture and throughout the writings of the Holy Fathers, there are a host of testimonies clearly showing that God punishes those who become involved with occultism and necromancy (seeking to speak with the dead). Our Saviour teaches us that "blessed are they that have not seen and yet have believed." The Apostle Paul shows us who believe in Christ that we must seek after the power of faith and not the perception of our material eyes, saying, "We walk by faith, not by sight." The prowling demons, however, instruct certain men not to be satisfied with the teaching of the Saviour and of His Apostle—that is, to walk with trust in the faith of Christ—but rather to seek, by every means, to view with their sensible eyes that which is accessible only to the eyes of faith. The man who resorts to black magic and necromancy is an enemy of God, diso-

Jn. 20:29

2 Cor. 5:7

bedient to His commandments, not content with the salvific lessons that God teaches him through the Scriptures—but rather, prompted by the demons in this illegitimate work, he seeks to investigate things rationally. And so, believing in these fantasies, he withdraws from God and from the teaching of our Church.

Those who concern themselves with this and call upon the spirits of the dead, bring in as support the example of Saul, who sought from the sorceress the invocation of the soul of Samuel. Those who have fallen into this delusion of Saul should know from his punishment that they are culpable before God. For, because of this very transgression, Saul lost his kingdom and his life and was punished by God to be killed with his own sword. The punishment of Saul for his unlawful conversing with the dead is related in Holy Scripture in this way: "So Saul died for his transgression which he committed against the LORD, even against the word of the LORD, which he kept not, and also for asking counsel of one that had a familiar spirit, to inquire of it; and inquired not of the LORD: therefore he slew him, and turned the kingdom unto David the son of Jesse."

In the Old Testament, the Lord commands the following: "Regard not them that have familiar spirits, neither seek after wizards, to be defiled by them: I am the LORD your God." And elsewhere: "A man or also woman that hath a familiar spirit, or that is a wizard, shall surely be put to death: they shall stone them with stones: their blood shall be upon them." The invocation of the spirits of the dead is hateful before God, Who has never given it sanction among His people: " . . . there shall not be found among you any one that maketh his son or his daughter to pass through the fire, or that useth divination, or an observer of times, or an enchanter, or a witch, or a charmer, or a consulter with familiar spirits,

1 Sam. 28

1 Chr. 10:13-14

Lev. 19:31

Lev. 20:27

Dt. 18:9-14

or a wizard, or a necromancer. For all that do these things are an abomination unto the LORD." God considers this abomination one of man's greatest revolts against His Will. We have no need to communicate with the dead, since God has revealed to us everything He knows to be necessary and beneficial for our salvation. For example, conversing with the dead is not able to prove to us that the souls of the dead live as they once lived in this present life. This reality of the next life is not news to us, since we know it from Divine Revelation and it is a matter of faith, without there being the need for research and examination with our bodily senses. Divine Revelation offers us every assurance of truth. If someone wants to inspect and feel this with their visible senses, it means placing in doubt the truths which were revealed by God. Furthermore, in these spiritual discourses, there is no assurance that the spirit of the dead that was called for will appear and speak, for the evil spirits—the demons—mimic the righteous spirits, as Saint Paul teaches us: "Satan himself

2 Cor. 11:14

is transformed into an angel of light." And the Evangelist John tells us the following: "Beloved, believe not every spirit,

1 Jn. 4:1-3

but test the spirits whether they are of God."

In addition to all of this, the Holy Fathers tell us that in the case of Saul and the witch, it was not the spirit of Samuel that appeared, but a demonic spirit that had supplanted the spirit of Samuel. Saint Gregory of Nyssa says that the spirit was so dreadful and hideous that the sorceress was frightened by it. Likewise, we see in the case of Adam, whom God had called to the height of theosis, that he was deluded by the Devil and, falling from the grace of God, hid himself with Eve. There are many examples in Scripture from which we know, that by the delusion of the Devil, death is inherited instead of life, the lie instead of the truth, and evil instead of good.

Due to the danger of deception from visions and dreams, some of the Holy Fathers did not accept any kind of dream before performing a very careful examination. Saint John of the Ladder says, "Whoever does not believe in visions and dreams is a spiritual philosopher," and also that when the demons of vainglory and pride tempt the weaker brothers with visions and dreams, they make them into "prophets."

Abbot of St. Catherine's Monastery on Mount Sinai (6th c.) & author of The Ladder of Divine Ascent.

INQ.: The fortune-tellers and enchanters say that Holy Scripture relates cases of the appearances of dead men and angels. They also say that since Scripture attests to our ability to communicate directly with the dead, it follows that conjuring spirits is not foreign to Christianity and, above all, is not something anti-Christian.

EC: It is true, indeed, that Holy Scripture relates to us the appearance of Moses and Elias during the transfiguration of the Saviour and, also, that after the crucifixion of Christ many dead were raised from the tombs. Scripture also attests to the appearance of angels, such as at the news of the birth of Saint John the Baptist as well as the birth of the Saviour Christ, at the Resurrection of the Lord. Likewise, scripture attests to the intervention of Angels in the service of certain of the righteous and the saints of the Old and New Testaments. They communicated with men either face to face or through dreams. However, these appearances did not happen by the will and invocation of men, but by the command of God. These appearances certify the immortality of their souls and their power to be revealed to men in exceptional ways; however, they do not support the prerogative of man to seek out contact with the dead.

Mat. 17:3

Mat. 27:52-53

Lk. 1:11-20

Lk. 2:9-15

Mat. 28:2-7

Mat. 1:20, 2:13

INQ.: In the Old Testament, necromancy was practiced, as is clear in the case of Saul and the sorceress and elsewhere. In the Christian Church, likewise, that which we call the supplication of saints and angels is practiced. At its base, this is nothing else but an invocation of righteous souls or a communication with the dead, with the aim of helping the living with their particular needs. On account of this, it is claimed that occultism or fortune-telling represents a scriptural teaching that, in practice, is recognized by the Church.

EC: The truth regarding Saul and the sorceress was clarified earlier. Concerning the entreaty of saints and angels, in no way is it the same as necromancy. In calling upon the saints and angels, we do not have the intention or pretension of speaking sensibly with them, of seeing them, of hearing their voice, or of having them appear before us perceptibly in order to reveal to us mysteries, which God has determined should remain hidden from man. We speak to the saints and angels in our prayer by means of our noetic (νοερός) eyes and by means of our faith, without the need to see or hear them sensibly.

The conjurors have the aim and the need to call upon the spirits of the dead (I believe, however, that, in fact, they are spirits of demons, which appear in the form of the spirits of the dead), in order that they may reveal to them certain secrets that relate to the future of the dead or other curiosities forbidden by the law of God. Listen to what Holy Scripture has to say: "And when they shall say unto you, seek unto the necromancers and unto the soothsayers, who chirp and who mutter, Shall not a people seek unto their God? On behalf of the living should they seek unto the dead? To the law and the testimony! If they speak not according to this word, for them there is no daybreak."

When the unmerciful rich man called upon Abraham to send Lazarus to the house of his father and to make known the situation in which he was found, in order to bring his brothers to repentance, Abraham answered him that, for the living, the revelation of the Law (Moses and the Prophets) was sufficient. Indeed, in the Divine Revelation that was given to us with Holy Scripture and Holy Tradition, we lack nothing in the way of knowing about our salvation, nor do we have need to seek from the dead—or better, the demons—something favourable to our salvation.

Is. 8:19-20

When God sends us a Prophet, and it is not revealed to us immediately, this means that he does not want to make other disclosures, knowing that they will not be profitable for us. When someone who prophesies is not from God, without a doubt he is from the Devil, as were the False Prophets referred to in Scripture. They announced false visions, vanities, and preposterous prophecies relative to the condition of their heart. When they actually do tell us the truth, we should not believe it, since they do not say it with the aim of benefitting anyone—but rather, from deceptiveness, they seek to lead us into delusion. Look at the girl with the unclean spirit of divination in the city of Philippi of Macedonia: everything that the evil spirit said through her mouth was true, and yet the Apostle Paul admonished it to keep silent, casting out the demonic spirit.

Acts 16:16-18

As was suggested earlier, with the supplication of the saints and angels, we are not curious about what we will see or what we will hear from them (materially speaking), like the magicians and fortune-tellers with their invocation of spirits. We seek from God, through the saints, that which He deigns to give us for our salvation, while the psychics and shamans seek from the demons that appear in the semblance of dead men that which they themselves want, and even this out of base curiosity.

If, however, by the command of God, one of the saints or angels wanted to appear to us in a material way, there is no transgression in this, for we did not desire this or seek after this. Yet, even in such cases, it is necessary for us to be very careful, humble, prudent, and full of the fear of God because, knowing that Satan also assumes the guise of an angel, it may well be a fantasy of the Devil. Of course, even when the vision is from God, it is better for us not to receive it. For if we do this with humility, God will not be sorrowful, because He knows that we are taking heed not to accept within us the wolf instead of the shepherd. We do not, indeed, have need of seeing the saints and angels, but only to pray with faith and internal vision. Saint Neilos the Ascetic says, "Blessed is that intellect which arrives at the point of worshipping God without giving shape to His form within itself."

INQ.: The occultists and necromancers allege that, according to the teaching of Scripture, being born again or returning to life is accepted by the Scriptures, as in the case recorded of the return of Elias in the person of Saint John the Baptist. The angel said about John: "And he shall go before Him in the spirit and power of Elias." And the Saviour says similar words about John: "And if ye will receive it, this is Elias, who was to come," in other words, he concerning whom it was revealed by the Prophets must come. Another time the disciples asked the Lord, "'Why then say the scribes that Elias must first come?' And Jesus answered and said unto them, 'Elias truly shall first come, and restore all things. But I say unto you that Elias is come already, and they knew him not, but have done unto him whatsoever they listed. Likewise shall also the Son of man suffer of them. Then the disciples understood that he spake unto them of John the Baptist." Consequently, John the Baptist is Elias who is to come again

Margin references:
2 Cor. 11:14-15
Lk. 1:17
Mat. 11:14
Mal. 4:4
Mat. 17:10-13

into the world. Therefore, Jesus Christ taught that there is a re-awakening or retrieval of life. Is this not the case?

EC: Truly, the Prophet Malachi did prophesy the appearance of Elias, however, this was not fulfilled prior to the birth of the Messiah. Rather, Elias will appear just before the coming of the great and illustrious day of the Lord and thereby signify the beginning of the end of the world.

Mal. 3:23

We should understand the Angel's words, that John will come "in the spirit and power of Elias," to mean that he will manifest the force of Elias—in his mission to the world and in his preaching of repentance—by his zeal, deeds, toils, and raiment.

2 Kg. 1:8

Mat. 11:14
Mat. 17:10-13

The words of the Saviour would seem, indeed, to support the return of Elias in the person of John and that it would happen then and not at the end of the world. Nevertheless, based on the spirit of the teaching of the Saviour, it is not possible for John to be identified with Elias, but only to resemble him. Lucid and unmistakable proof of this is the fact that—to the question of the Jews of Jerusalem, which was addressed to John through the priests and Levites, regarding whether or not he was Elias—he categorically answered them, "I am not." It is impossible that John would contradict the Saviour and deny his identification with Elias. Furthermore, if Elias was to come in the person of John the Baptist, how was it that he appeared together with Moses on Mount Tabor during the Transfiguration of the Lord?

Jn. 1:21

Mat. 17:3

The regeneration which the Saviour speaks of to Nicodemos is not a bodily restoration but a spiritual rebirth from above through water and the spirit—that is, through Holy Baptism. The text itself rules out any possibility of a bodily rebirth, as Nicodemos had mistakenly understood, when it stresses that it is not speaking of a second bodily or natural birth.

Jn. 3:3-7

And yet, neither can the prudent mind accept the possibility of identifying John with that Prophet who is to come, Elias. Likewise, disagreeable is that which the spiritualists teach: namely, that his return happens for the purpose of moral purification and perfection, since Elias has no need of purification and moral perfecting. According to the Christian teaching, there does exist a return of the soul to the body—but only once—which occurs at the end of the world when all will be raised and the material body will be transfigured in order to participate in eternal life.

Jn. 9:2

INQ.: In relation to this, I found a passage in Holy Scripture difficult to understand. It is the passage which tells the story of the man born blind, who washed and was healed in the pool of Siloam. The Apostles asked the Lord, saying, "Master, who sinned, this man or his parents, that he was born blind?" It seems to follow from this that, apparently, the blind man was in a position to pay off those personal sins committed before his birth. This is what certain occultists and those who believe in reincarnation maintain.

Jn. 9:3

EC: As we said earlier, at the end of the world there will be one re-establishment of soul and body before the final judgement. This forgiveness of personal sins, or of the sins of the parents of the blind man, is something else entirely. The case of the man born blind is not concerned with who sinned and punished the blind man, as the Apostles mistakenly supposed. Rather, the Saviour brushed aside this opinion of theirs, saying that the man was not blind on account of his sins, but so that the "works of God should be made manifest in him," or so that His therapeutic power may be made manifest. In the teachings of Christ, nowhere does there exist, even in this life, punishment as the fruit of a just reward. The loosing and forgiveness of sins occur in this life as well. However, the definitive loosing from the shackles of sin happens after the Future Judgement, when it will be not for purification but as a recompense. Redemption came from the Lord alone for the sake of all mankind, and no one, by any means whatsoever, is able to forgive his own sins.

As for the other teachings of the spiritualists, like those presented earlier, they are all anti-Christian and their musk has been removed under the scrutiny of the teaching of our Orthodox Church. Our Church teaches us that:

1) Souls have been created directly by God.

2) According to the teaching of our Church, under no circumstances can one speak of the pre-existence of souls.

3) Bodies are creations of God and not of the angels.

4) The place of punishment is Hell [Greek: Gehenna], in which the conditions are immutable—something certified by the words of Divine Revelation.

5) The demons cannot be saved.

6) There exists only one resurrection and return of the soul to the resurrected body, which will happen at the end of the world for the final judgement.

No one among the race of men can compel a soul to leave Paradise and go to hell, or vice versa, as the deluded spiritualists believe. How can such a thing happen when we know very well that the souls of the just are in the hands of God? Likewise, we also know that between the living and the dead, "a great gulf is fixed" and no one from there is able

Lk. 16:26

to come to us here. Do you think it possible for one among men to take a soul from the hand of God against His Will and to request it to engage in a conversation? Can someone cross that impassable chasm referred to in the Gospel and, through an invocation, bring a soul from the other world to earth? And if we assume that we are benefitted by such a medium, how can we accept it, knowing that it is hateful and an abhorrence to God?

Dt. 18:9-13

Someone might say that, indeed, the souls of the just are in the hands of God; however, the spiritualists, in their meetings, do not call upon souls of the righteous, but of the wicked, who are not in the hands of God, but in Hades.

Are the souls of the branded and accursed found beyond the supervision of God? Listen to what the Lord says in the Revelation of Saint John with reference to this: "Fear not; I am the first and the last: I am he that liveth, and was dead; and, behold, I am alive for evermore, Amen; and have the keys of hell and of death."

See also note 1 on page 217

Rev. 1:17-18

Consequently, just as the souls of the righteous are in the hand of God, so too, those of the wicked in the kingdom of Hades are also under the infinite and indescribable authority of God. They are not to be found at the disposal of certain spiritualists who would like to call upon them to serve them in their lawless work. If, through the medium, spirits appear which they have called, let them know that these are not the spirits of relatives or friends. On the contrary, they are the unclean spirits of darkness. Until the last judgement, God has left these demons free to harass men and to reside in—according to the witness of Holy Scripture—the uppermost stratum of the atmosphere, of the "high places." Against these powers and principalities, the Christians battle with the weapons God has given them.

Eph. 6:12

Eph. 6:11, 13-17

INQ.: Could you give us a brief summary of the teaching of those who occupy themselves with the occult, who are variously called spiritualists, fortune-tellers, sorcerers, necromancers, etc.?

EC: The teaching of the spiritualists takes many forms, according to the testimonies of the vanguard of occultism. Here it is in general terms:

1) They deny the dogma of the Holy Trinity, replacing it with one supreme god and other solar-gods considered his sons or with other planets that they compare with the Holy Spirit, and all of it is organized hierarchically.

2) Some speculate that God is not the creator of the cosmos, but only its organizer.

3) They say that Jesus is a higher spirit and our sun's god, who guides man but does not save him. They believe that the true revelation comes from the spirits that appear to man by means of the medium.

4) They believe that man is made of flesh and encircled with the spirit and that the soul of man has a casing or husk, which can leave the visible world and communicate after death, with those of the living who are worthy and believing.

5) They say that salvation is accomplished with the evolution toward the good and with reincarnation. They accept an infinite god having under his authority other, lesser, gods, who govern particular planets and areas of heaven, assisted by the angels. Spirits of planets, animals, and sentient beings inhabit the universe. The body of man

is destroyed, but the shell and spirit is immortal. Human beings that are good have within them the good spirit, while the evil pass over into another body until they also, themselves, become good and so on.

Tree of Life Cross

Pen and ink, by Scott Patrick O'Rourke (https://orthodoxartsjournal.org/scott-patrick-orourke/).

FOR FURTHER READING

Romanian Elders and Hesychast Tradition

Arch. Ioanichie Balan, *Shepherd of Souls: Elder Cleopa the New Hesychast of Romania.* Platina, CA, 96076: St. Herman of Alaska Brotherhood.

Bishop Seraphim Joanta, *Romania: Its Hesychast Tradition & Culture.* Platina, CA, 96076: St. Herman of Alaska Brotherhood.

Catechetical Works

St. Innocent of Moscow, *Indication of the Way into the Kingdom of Heaven.* Jordanville, NY, 13361: Holy Trinity Monastery. 2013

New-Martyr Archbishop Ilarion, *Christianity or the Church?* Jordanville, NY, 13361: Holy Trinity Monastery.

Fr. George Metallinos, *The Way: An Introduction to the Orthodox Faith.* Meteora, Greece: Holy Meteora Publications.

Eusebius, *The History of the Church.* New York, NY 10014: Penguin Books. 1989

Blessed Theophylact, *The Explanation of the New Testament.* House Springs, MO, 63051: Chrysostom Press (distributed by St. Herman of Alaska Brotherhood).

St. John of San Francisco, *Orthodox Veneration of the Mother of God.* Platina, CA, 96076: St. Herman of Alaska Brotherhood. 2004.

Anonymous Pilgrim, *The Way of a Pilgrim.* Florence, AZ 85132: St. Anthony's Greek Orthodox Monastery Press. 2019

St. Seraphim of Sarov, *Wonderful Revelation to the World: St. Seraphim of Sarov's Conversation with Motovilov*. Florence, AZ 85132: St. Anthony's Greek Orthodox Monastery Press. 2021

Fr. Seraphim Rose, *God's Revelation to the Human Heart*. Platina, CA, 96076: St. Herman of Alaska Brotherhood. 1997

Fr. Seraphim Rose, *Orthodoxy & the Religion of the Future*. Platina, CA, 96076: St. Herman of Alaska Brotherhood. 2004

Archbishop Averky, *The Epistles and the Apocalypse*. Jordanville, NY, 13361: Holy Trinity Monastery. 2018

Jordan Badjis, *Common Ground: An Introduction to Eastern Christianity for the American Christian*. Minneapolis, MN, 55424: Light and Life Publishing Company.

Writings of the Church Fathers

St. Athanasius the Great, *On the Incarnation*. Florence, AZ 85132: St. Anthony's Greek Orthodox Monastery Press. 2021

St. Basil of Caesarea, *On the Holy Spirit*. Florence, AZ 85132: St. Anthony's Greek Orthodox Monastery Press. 2021

St. Irenaeus, *Against Heresies: Book One*. Washington, DC, 20064: CUA Press.

St. John of Damascus, *Exact Exposition of the Orthodox Faith*. Florence, AZ 85132: St. Anthony's Greek Orthodox Monastery Press. 2019

St. John of Damascus, *On the Divine Images*. Crestwood, NY, 10707: Saint Vladimir's Seminary. 2003

The Sayings of the Desert Fathers: Florence, AZ 85132: St. Anthony's Greek Orthodox Monastery Press. 2019

Lives of Modern Saints

Archimandrite Lazarus Moore, *An Extraordinary Peace: Saint Seraphim, Flame of Sarov.* Port Townsned, WA, 98368: Anaphora Press. 2009

Sotos Chondropoulos, *St. Nektarios: A Saint for our Times.* Brookline, MA, 02445: Holy Cross Orthodox Press. 1997

Fr. Seraphim Rose, *Saint John the Wonderworker.* Platina, CA, 96076: St. Herman of Alaska Brotherhood.

St. Paisius of the Holy Mountain, *Saint Arsenios of Cappadocia.* Souroti, Greece: Monastery of St. John the Theologian.

Elder Ephraim of Philotheou and Arizona, *My Elder Joseph the Hesychast.* Florence, AZ, 85232: St. Anthony's Monastery. 2021

Elder Isaac, *Elder Paisios of Mount Athos.* Vatopedi, Greece: St. Arsenios the Cappadocian Monastery. 2009

Dogmatic Theology and History

Fr. John Romanides, *Patristic Theology.* Thessaloniki, Greece: Uncut Mountain Press. 2022

R.S. Haugh, General Editor, *The Collected Works of George Florovsky.* Belmont, MA, 02178: Notable & Academic Books.

Fr. Michael Pomazansky, *Orthodox Dogmatic Theology: A Concise Exposition.* Translated by Fr. Seraphim Rose. Platina, CA, 96076: St. Herman of Alaska Brotherhood. 2005

Aristeides Papadakis, *The Christian East and the Rise of the Papacy: The Church 1071-1453.* Yonkers, NY, 10707: St. Vladimir's Seminary Press.

SCRIPTURAL INDEX

UNCUT MOUNTAIN PRESS TITLES

Books by Archpriest Peter Heers

Fr. Peter Heers, *The Ecclesiological Renovation of Vatican II: An Orthodox Examination of Rome's Ecumenical Theology Regarding Baptism and the Church*, 2015

Fr. Peter Heers, *The Missionary Origins of Modern Ecumenism: Milestones Leading up to 1920*, 2007

The Works of our Father Among the Saints, Nikodemos The Hagiorite

Vol. 1: *Exomologetarion: A Manual of Confession*
Vol. 2: *Concerning Frequent Communion of the Immaculate Mysteries of Christ*
Vol. 3: *Confession of Faith*

Other Available Titles

Elder Cleopa of Romania, *The Truth of our Faith, Vol. II: Discourses from Holy Scripture on the Holy Mysteries*

Fr. John Romanides, *Patristic Theology: The University Lectures of Fr. John Romanides*

Archimandrite Ephraim Triandaphillopoulos, *Noetic Prayer as the Basis of Mission and the Struggle Against Heresy*

G.M. Davis, *Antichrist: The Fulfillment of Globalization - The Ancient Church and the End of History*

Robert Spencer, *The Church and the Pope*

Select Forthcoming Titles

St. Gregory Palamas, *Apodictic Treatise on the Procession of the Holy Spirit*

The Lives and Witness of 20th Century Athonite Fathers

Protopresbyter Anastasios Gotsopoulos, *On Common Prayer with the Heterodox, According to the Canons of the Church*

The New Martyr St. Hilarion Troitsky, *An Overview of the History of the Dogma Concerning the Church*

Elder George of Grigoriou, *Catholicism*

Let No One Fear Death - Collection of essays from Orthodox leaders reflecting on Covidism

Nicholas Baldimtsis, *Life and Witness of St. Iakovos of Evia*

Georgio Kassir, *Errors of the Latins*

This 4th Edition of

THE TRUTH OF OUR FAITH

translated by Fr. Peter Heers, with a foreword by
Archimandrite Joseph, Abbot of the Holy Monastery of
Xeropotamou on Mt. Athos, and a new cover design by
Michael Jackson, typeset in Adobe Garamond Pro, and
printed through HolyOrthodoxBooks.com in
this two thousandeth and twenty second year
of our Lord's Holy Incarnation, is one of the many fine
titles available from Uncut Mountain Press, translators
and publishers of Orthodox Christian theological and
spiritual literature. Find the book you are looking for at

www.uncutmountainpress.com

GLORY BE TO GOD
FOR ALL THINGS

AMEN.